Exiled Memories

Exiled ❖ Memories

A Cuban Childhood

By Pablo Medina

 University of Texas Press, Austin

Copyright © 1990 by the University of Texas Press
All rights reserved
Printed in the United States of America

First Edition, 1990

Requests for permission to reproduce material from this work should be sent to
Permissions, University of Texas Press, Box 7819, Austin, Texas 78713-7819.

∞ The paper used in this publication meets the minimum requirements of
American National Standard for Information Sciences — Permanence of Paper for
Printed Library Materials, ANSI Z39.48-1984.

Earlier versions of parts of this work were published in *Confrontation*, 1984
("Arrival"), *The Antioch Review*, 1985 ("Grandfather Pablo"), and *Linden Lane
Magazine*, 1985 ("Mina" and "El Guayabal").

Library of Congress Cataloging-in-Publication Data
Medina, Pablo, 1948–
    Exiled memories : a Cuban childhood / by Pablo Medina. — 1st ed.
        p.   cm.
    ISBN 0-292-77636-5 (alk. paper)
    1. Medina, Pablo, 1948–   — Biography — Youth.   2. Poets, American — 20th
century — Biography — Youth. 3. Cuba — Social life and customs.   4. Cuban
Americans — Biography.   I. Title.
PS3563.E24Z465   1990
811'.54 — dc20
[B]   90-30376
                                                                               CIP

For my parents, Pablo and Bela,
and for the family

. . . the child who had experienced
that happiness existed no longer, it was
like a reminiscence of somebody else.
— L. Tolstoi, "The Death of Ivan Ilych"

Contents

Preface

AN OLD TEACHER of mine once told me that a serious book ought to have a preface. Not being one to challenge the wisdom of an experienced, if dogmatic, man of letters, I set for myself the goal of writing a preface that might serve as a lantern for the reader. What higher purpose than this for a writer: to concern himself with the welfare of those who ventured into his book? But, alas, hard as I thought, slavishly as I read and reread the essays that make up these memoirs, I could not wean the great unifying element, the High Thesis, from them.

In the grip of dejection, I almost abandoned the project and let the reader flounder about listlessly to discover the essence of these pages alone.

But no. A preface I would have, even if it killed me or the reader, my fellow companion in this voyage. I changed my approach. I would no longer attempt to treat theme, but rather my reasons for composing these memoirs, of which there are as many as there is one: I felt like it.

Now that I have gotten that off my chest, I can offer a few clarifications. I did not always feel like it. As happens with everything I write, I often wanted to give it up. At times I did — temporarily — that I might visit a friend or write a poem or two or dream of a pretty girl I might have met. Coming home, I found the page still rolled into the typewriter refusing to give up. Let me say, then, that I felt like it most of the time.

The second clarification has to do with a more public but no

less egotistical matter. On visiting my great-aunt and my grandmother several summers ago, I was awakened to the fact that they
and the other old folks of the family would not live forever, and
that the long twilight of their lives would soon come to an end.
When they went, they would take with them the myths and
folklore I had grown up with. That, I thought, should never be
allowed to happen. And who better than I, who was born in
the midst of this soup, simmered in it, then plucked violently
away, to chronicle our past for those generations who had never
lived it?

Third clarification (and, I promise, the last): This book is a
record of my Odyssey, my return to Ithaca. Life in the United
States for me has not been a search for roots (that presumes their
loss), but rather a quixotic attempt to become a creature I never
was nor can ever be: an American as I understood, or misun-
derstood, it to be. I thought that changing nationalities was as
easy as changing clothes, speech patterns, books to read. Twenty
years (well, twenty-four) of wanderings taught me that national-
ity is in the soul, if it is anywhere, and to change that requires
much more than window dressing of one's body or tongue or
mind. The Americanization I sought for so long required the an-
nihilation of memory, that tireless lady who is forever weaving
and unweaving her multicolored tapestries. I don't believe anyone can do that by natural means.

Nor do I wish to delude myself that I am immaculately Cuban.
I left the country of my birth at twelve, too young an age not to be
thoroughly influenced and changed by a new environment. That
new land, and my responses to it, however, is the subject of another, as yet unwritten, book.

Exiled Memories

Leaving; we tried our best to smile (1960).

SNOW. EVERYWHERE THE snow and air so cold it cracks and my words hang stiffly in the air like cartoons. After that first stunning welcome of the New York winter, I rush down the steps of the plane and sink my bare hands into the snow, press it into a ball, and throw it at my sister. I miss by a few yards. The snowball puffs on the ground. I make another and miss again. Then I can make no more, for my hands are numb. I look down at them: red and wet, they seem disembodied, no longer mine. A few flakes land on them, but these flakes are not the ones I know from *Little LuLu* or *Archie;* they are big lumpy things that melt soon after landing. On closer look, I can make out the intricate crystals, small and furry and short lived. As if from a great distance, I hear my mother calling. Her voice seems changed by the cold and the words come quicker, in shorter bursts, as if there might be a limited supply of them. I follow the family into the airport building. It is early February. It is El Norte.

The drive into Manhattan is a blur. We piled into a cab and took a wide and busy highway in, most probably the Grand Central Parkway. Once over the East River, my first impression was of riding down into a canyon, much of it shadowy and forbidding, where the sky, steel gray at the time, was a straight path like the street we were on, except bumpier and softer: old cotton swabbed in mercury. It seemed odd that out of that ominous ceiling came the pure white snow I had just touched.

But the snow on the ground did not stay white very long. Nothing does in New York. It started graying at the edges four days after our arrival when my father took my sister and me to school, Robert F. Wagner Junior High, on East 72nd Street. It was a long brick building that ran the length of the block. Inauspicious, blank, with shades half-raised on the windows, it could have been a factory or a prison. Piled to the side of the entrance steps was a huge mound of snow packed with children like fruit on supermarket ice. J.H.S. 167 was a typical New York school, a microcosm of the city where all races mingled and fought and, on occasion, learned. The halls were crowded, the classes were crowded, even the bathroom during recess was packed to capacity.

On that first day I was witness to a scene that was to totally alter my image of what school was. On my way from one class to the next, I saw a teacher — who, I later learned, was the prefect of discipline — dragging a girl away by the arm. The girl, trying to tug herself free, was screaming, "Mother fucker, mother fucker." He slapped her across the face several times. Most students, already practicing the indifference that is the keynote of survival in New York, barely turned their heads. I, however, stared, frozen by violence in a place previous experience had deluded me into thinking ought to be quiet and genteel and orderly. It was the loud ring of the bell directly overhead that woke me. I was late for English class.

When I entered the room, the teacher, a slightly pudgy lady with silver white hair, asked if I had a pass. I did not know what a pass was but I answered no anyway. It was my first day and I had gotten lost in the halls.

"Well, in that case, young man, you may come in."

She spoke with rounded vowels and smooth, slightly slurred *r*'s rolling out of her mouth from deep in the throat. Years later I was to learn to identify this manner of speech as an affectation of the educated.

"Next time, however, you must have a pass."

Not that it mattered if one was late to English class. Much of the time was spent doing reading or writing assignments while Mrs. Gall, whose appearance belied that she was close to retirement, did crossword puzzles. A few days later, in fact, something happened that endeared me to her for the rest of the term. Speaking to herself, not expecting any of the students to help her, she said, "A nine letter word for camel." Almost instantaneously, as if by magic, I responded, "Dromedary."

She looked up at me. "That's very good. You have a nice complexion. Where are you from?"

"Complexion?" I asked.

"Yes, skin."

Skin? What does skin have to do with any of this? I had never thought of my skin, let alone considered it a mark of foreignness.

"Cuba."

"Ah, I was there once."

Then she went off on a monologue of beaches and nightlife and weather.

Home for now was a two-bedroom apartment in a residential hotel on East 86th Street, which we would not have been able to afford were it not for the graces of the company my father worked for. We had few clothes, little money, and no possessions to speak of, yet I do not remember ever lacking anything, except perhaps good food, as my mother, who as a middle-class housewife had always relied on maids in Cuba, was just beginning to learn how to cook.

If there was no money for expensive restaurants or theater tickets, I always had thirty cents for the subway fare. From this building that glossed our poverty, I set out into the city that lay open like a geometric flower of concrete and steel. Its nectar was bittersweet, but it kept me, us, from wallowing in the self-pity and stagnation that I have seen among so many exiles. After a few months, realizing that a return to the island was not forthcoming, we looked on a future where the sun was rising again. Not the fierce tropical sun that made everything jump with life and set over the palm trees as quickly as it had risen, but a gentler, slower sun that yielded reluctantly to night and promised to renew itself. Constancy. It was blonde.

The New York sun is not ubiquitous. It hides behind buildings until well after eleven, then appears and disappears for a few hours in the grid sky. Eventually one does not see it at all, only its afterglow diffused by smog and its reflection on the windows of the tallest buildings. Manhattan is an island without sunrise or sunset. If you want to witness the former, you go to the Long Island shore and look toward Europe; if you want the latter, you move west.

And so it was. I could go nowhere but into the city. Sometimes alone, sometimes with Sam, the one friend I made at school, I traveled from one end of the city to the other. At first boredom was the motivator, but soon an intense curiosity that my parents not only tolerated but encouraged became the fire that fueled me.

Thus I discovered Washington Square, the source of Fifth Avenue. Elegant, restrained, neo-Parisian, and ebbing southward from it, Greenwich Village, already in decadence but nevertheless glowing with an odd sort of peripheral, rebellious energy. Some seed had sprouted there I sensed, but it was years before I saw its vines spread throughout the land.

North I went, too, to find the Avenue's mouth and realized that this was no river of gold, but a snake that devoured its own and spewed them back to a place beyond light or hope or future. When one sees Harlem at 125th Street and Fifth Avenue, one comes face to face with the worst despair. The people there are fixed in a defeat not of their making, but rather the result of the color of their skins and a heritage imposed on them from the outside. Black you are and poor you shall remain; black you are and damned you shall be. The Avenue begins in Paris and ends in hell.

In six months we moved to 236th Street in the Upper Bronx, this time to a modest apartment in a modest building. The trees on the streets actually looked like trees, not like stunted saplings. They gave shade; there was enough room on their trunks to carve initials and love notes; the streets were not forever clogged with traffic; the sun was more visible, and from our sixth-floor windows the red blood of the sunset spilled over the Hudson a mile away.

Discovering the installment plan, my parents bought furniture and china and pictures to put on the walls. We even got a stereo. We met other families in the building, formed friendships. We were, suddenly, in middle-class mainstream America, Bronx style, and the past released its grip and ebbed far enough away so that only memory could reach it. Somehow luck had graced us: we had circumvented the snake.

From left: Carlos, Juana María, and my father, Pablo II (1925).

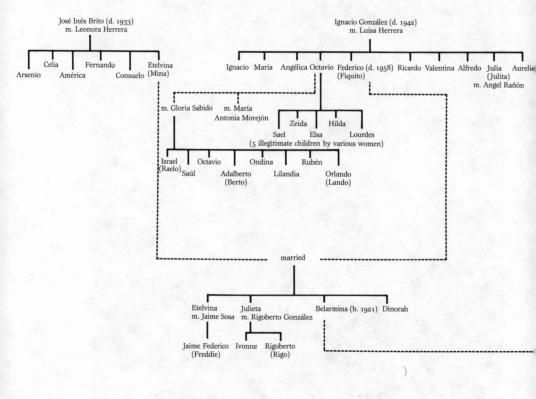

José Inés Brito (d. 1933)
m. Leonora Herrera

Arsenio
Celia
América
Fernando
Consuelo
Etelvina
(Mina)

Ignacio González (d. 1942)
m. Luisa Herrera

Ignacio   María   Angélica   Octavio   Federico (d. 1958)   Ricardo   Valentina   Alfredo   Julia   Aureli
(Fiquito)   (Julita)
                                                                                             m. Angel Rañón

m. Gloria Sabido   m. María
                     Antonia Morejón

Zeida   Hilda

Sael   Elsa   Lourdes
(5 illegitimate children by various women)

Israel
(Raelo)   Octavio   Ondina   Rubén
      Saúl   Adalberto   Lilandia   Orlando
                  (Berto)   (Lando)

married

Etelvina   Julieta
m. Jaime Sosa   m. Rigoberto González   Belarmina (b. 1921)   Dinorah

Jaime Federico   Ivonne   Rigoberto
(Freddie)   (Rigo)

)

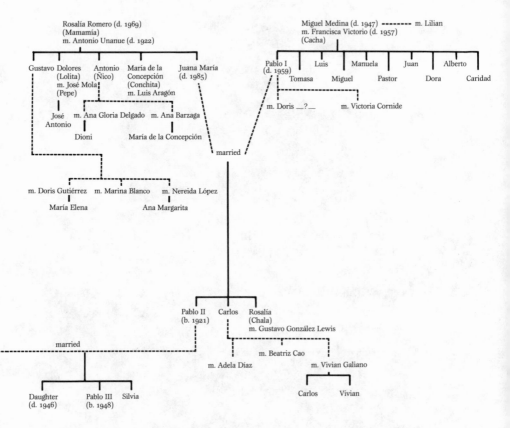

Rosalía Romero (d. 1969)
(Mamamía)
m. Antonio Unanue (d. 1922)

Miguel Medina (d. 1947) -------- m. Lilian
m. Francisca Victorio (d. 1957)
(Cacha)

Gustavo Dolores   Antonio   María de la   Juana María
         (Lolita)   (Ñico)   Concepción   (d. 1985)
         m. José Mola   (Conchita)
         (Pepe)   m. Luis Aragón

Pablo I   Luis   Manuela   Juan   Alberto
(d. 1959)
         Tomasa   Miguel   Pastor   Dora   Caridad

José   m. Ana Gloria Delgado   m. Ana Barzaga
Antonio

m. Doris __?__   m. Victoria Cornide

         Dioni   María de la Concepción

married

m. Doris Gutiérrez   m. Marina Blanco   m. Nereida López

María Elena   Ana Margarita

Pablo II   Carlos   Rosalía
(b. 1921)   (Chala)
                      m. Gustavo González Lewis

married

                  m. Beatriz Cao

         m. Adela Díaz   m. Vivian Galiano

Daughter   Pablo III   Silvia
(d. 1946)   (b. 1948)

                              Carlos   Vivian

Luis Aragón at the height of his career (early 1940s).

"La Bolsa del Saber" on the air. Facing the camera seated at far right is Grandfather Pablo. Asking the question is Luis Aragón (1940).

Miguel Medina (ca. 1918).

Grandfather Pablo contemplating Toscanini, or vice versa (1953).

Grandfather Fiquito getting a haircut (1940).

Mamamía's house before a hurricane (1950).

Mamamía's house after a hurricane (1950).

Juana María, my sister, and I (1950).

Mamamía, Lolita, and Conchita in mourning (ca. 1923).

La Luisa

CUBA HAS A province named Matanzas, after a series of slaughters perpetrated by Spanish soldiers on the Indians of the area. The province, east of Havana, stretches toward the center of the island and is considered to be among the most fertile. Endless fields of sugarcane, interrupted occasionally by sugar mills and towns, simmer in the sun like green fire. To the south, hills and valleys meld into what is referred to by geographers as the Llanura Roja (the Red Plain). The ground there is blood red. Toward the lower edge of the Llanura my grandfather had his *colonia*, La Luisa.

An interesting term, *colonia*. It is derived directly from the Latin word meaning farm or settlement; but in Cuba it was a throwback to the period after the Ten Years' War (1868–1878), when, with the end of slavery, sugar mills were forced to parcel out their landholdings to sugar farmers called *colonos*. At first the *colonos* were little more than indentured farmers, having to give the sugar mill a substantial portion of their harvest. With time, however, the *colonos* thrived on the land, and eventually their descendants identified more with the island that gave them birth than with the distant Spanish lion. Out of this homegrown race, the creoles, came many revolutionaries who helped liberate the country from the grip of monarchy and colonialism. This same revolutionary tradition, born out of the creoles' need to find an identity as a people, crested in 1959 when the word *colonia* at last became an archaism in the fullest sense. Farms in Cuba are now known as "agricultural cooperatives."

La Luisa lay between two towns on the southern circuit of the Carretera Central, the main highway that ran the length of the island. In the north was Pedro Betancourt, formerly known as Corral Falso, where my grandparents had their townhouse; to the south, beyond Jardines, a *colonia* owned by my great-uncle Octavio and his countless sons, was a smaller town, Torrientes. Farther east and south was Jagüey Grande, the last town before Zapata Swamp, a vast area bare of human habitation but for the shacks of the *carboneros* (charcoal makers), semiwild people who eked out a living by selling charcoal to nearby farmers.

I would spend summers and winter vacations at the *colonia.* When my parents couldn't drive me, they would send me in a *botero,* a collective taxi that followed the route from Havana to Pedro Betancourt. One of my earliest memories is of one of these rides. Besides myself and the driver Zacarías, there was a black family of five who were on their way to visit relatives in the country. The only one of them who stands out clearly in my mind now is the patriarch. He wore a white guayabera and white pants that contrasted sharply with his coal black skin. He was wrinkled, very wrinkled, as if the river of life had once flowed through him and now only its dried-out imprint remained, and he smelled of molasses and lime. Somewhere in Matanzas, far from any town, the car broke down. Zacarías tinkered awhile with the motor but returned saying he didn't know what was wrong. The grandfather got out mumbling through his toothless mouth something about *despojo.* He looked around and headed to a bush from which he broke a branch. With it he drew an imaginary circle on the road around the car, then brushed the motor with the leaves. Next he took a white handkerchief from his back pocket, pulled it taut, spit on it, crumpled it, pulled it taut and spit on it again, then spread it carefully over the carburetor. *"Dale,"* he said to the driver who was now sitting dejectedly in the car smoking a cigarette. The driver raised his hand in disdain but obeyed. The car gurgled once, twice, and finally the motor roared. The old man had fixed it without once touching the insides. We reached our destination inside an hour.

Once a large front garden with many flowering bushes stretched from the house to a stone wall by the railroad tracks, but I barely remember that. Eminent domain had been invoked by government engineers and the highway was built right through the garden. Not that my grandparents minded. Getting in and out of La Luisa had been, before the road appeared, a slow and arduous process, and during heavy rain it was impossible, except on horseback. The house itself was a purely functional wood frame structure with floor-to-ceiling windows that allowed the breeze to cool the interior even on the hottest summer afternoon. The floor was concrete slab painted red, making for easy cleaning. In the back, behind the bedrooms that opened railroad style onto an exposed hallway, were the kitchen, a large pantry, and the charcoal storage room. A wooden gate led to the backyard where my world started.

For La Luisa was a place that belonged to the outside: to the animals, the trees, the sugarcane, the fierce sun and the fierce rain, the soft dusk and the soul-quiet evenings where the sounds of the modern world rarely, if ever, intruded. For me, it was a place of learning and experience, the crucible where humans and nature blended, where sweat gave forth fruit, where the wind whinnied, the moon mooed, and owls whooshed through the night; where luck was as much a good cane harvest as getting out of bed in the morning without stepping on a scorpion.

Farmers like my grandfather, Fiquito, were totally dependent on the whims of the outside, living always on the edge. Hard work mattered, but so did luck, fortune, fate, whatever you want to call it. He went out to the fields at six in the morning just before dawn, returned at noon for dinner, and went out again at three until the sun touched the top of the farthest trees. That was time enough to reach home before dark. Routine helped luck along, nursed it, treated it as a member of the family.

Fortune, however, will turn, as a trusted dog will turn and strike its master. A hurricane, an arsonist's fire, or a fall in sugar prices could ruin a man. Nothing to do then but start over, and never mind that luck had turned against you. You were alive, weren't you, and healthy? You still had a family; you still had the land, rich and red and ready. Above all, you had yourself, for you were the land. It was your birth, your growth, and your death.

Not to realize this was to be no man on the earth, bound to fail as a *colono*. If he ever taught me anything, Fiquito showed me in his life that no one is any better than anyone else; it is just that good fortune like good rain will fall in one spot and not another and may stop as suddenly as it comes.

My grandfather, true farmer that he was, loved the land not in a patriotic sense, but rather as a son. Thus, his unquestioning devotion to it and his confidence when working it. Fiquito could know no other life because he knew no other place. His country was the earth and he dealt not with principles and ideals but with planting and harvesting and the ever present cycles of life and death. In retrospect, all of us who knew him are relieved that he died one year before the Castro take-over. Not that the land would have been taken from him as it was taken from grandfather Mina, but he would have been taken from the land, losing that vital connection to existence that made him admirable as a person. Better off dead of cancer than to have had the hurricane of fate pull him up by his roots and fling him to a netherworld of concrete, artificial lights, and hands that grasp at empty air for something to hold on to and find not even their own shadows. Even in his final delirium, Fiquito talked of the land, urging his son-in-law to saddle his horse and unlock the gate so he could leave without delay. He died a lucky man.

La Luisa was a primitive place. It wasn't until the mid-fifties that my grandfather bought his first electric generator. Before then, gaslight and kerosene lamps were the only sources of light at night. Evenings after supper, we would sit on the front porch under the dim flicker of the gas burner, talking, watching the absolute darkness that surrounded our bubble of light. I remember the soft buzz of the flame and the faint sulfurous smell. At around ten o'clock, the two pellets dropped into the canister that fed the system gave out and we all went to bed.

Cooking was done on a charcoal stove. Fiquito would start the fire at five in the morning and make coffee. At five-thirty or six, he came to my bed with a steaming cup. At home, I resented being awakened early; in La Luisa waking was a special treat I looked forward to. Fresh Cuban coffee made from beans grown in the garden and sweetened with raw sugar is a drink excelled by few. When it is offered at first hint of dawn, held by the hand that plucked the beans, spread them out in the sun to dry, and ground them, it is a nectar the gods would envy.

Soon after coffee and his breakfast of a raw egg dropped into a glass of sweet sherry, Fiquito would mount his horse that Domingo the foreman had readied, and the two would head out for a day's work.

Out in the fields, the cane cutters huddled in small groups, fingering their razor sharp machetes; the oxcarts that carried the cut cane to the railroad depot were lined single file, and the *carreteros* (teamsters) kept the oxen in line with a mixture of curses and caresses. This was the time when it was light enough for them to inspect their animals for ticks, cuts, bruises, and the fit of their yokes, and they did this with much the same intent attitude one sees in the faces of modern day truckdrivers checking their rigs. Once Fiquito and Domingo arrived, the work started. The men gathered along the length of the field to cut and slash at the cane, one stalk at a time. They held the stalk midway up with the left hand, then swung the machete to cut the cane three inches above the ground. They cleared the stalk of chaff, held their machetes head high and somewhat to the left, then swung the cane toward the blade and released it as it was cut in two. The pieces twirled in the air and landed on a mound behind each man. The whole process took two or three seconds. As soon as there was enough cane, the first wagon was loaded and sent off to the depot where the load was transferred to railroad cars for its trip to the sugar mill. After the first hour or so of work, a steady stream of oxcart traffic flowed in and out of the field. It was a noisy undertaking. *Carreteros* screamed at the oxen; the oxen mooed and bellowed, protesting the prods their masters applied to their rumps. The more they protested, the more they were prodded. Domingo's voice, gravelly and tough like a stretched sinew, threw itself at the cane cutters. And under it all was the constant chomp of the machetes as they bit into the ripe cane.

Fiquito sat proudly on his horse. He paced up and down the line, never raising his voice, watching the *macheteros'* work, directing them this way and that, calling for a break when he thought the men needed it. With white guayabera, jodphurs, handmade riding boots, and a Stetson hat he had bought in the capital, he was the embodiment of the benevolent but firm *caudillo*. To further emphasize his authority, he carried a .38-caliber revolver with an ivory handle. At the time, I did not understand why he always wore it in the field. I never once saw him fire the gun, not even for practice. When I grew older, well after he was dead, I tried to reject men like my grandfather because they represented the exploitation of the poor and downtrodden. But I could never dismiss Fiquito directly. He was kind, well mannered, and as fair a man as I have ever met. He paid well by the standards of the time. He provided housing for his workers and a small plot of land for those with families; when they were sick, he took care of them. But as I said, La Luisa was a primitive place. Violence, especially among the itinerant cane cutters, was commonplace. When the heat of midmorning bore down on them, they would take off their shirts, and I saw long scars on the backs, chests, and arms of some of them — the results of Saturday night drunken brawls. Lucky they who had not lost a limb. These men were wild and untutored, and they worked like dogs. They also had short tempers, an understandable trait given the brutal nature of their work. Fiquito's attitude and the respect he inspired in many of them kept them with their minds on the cutting. The gun was there just in case. Would he have used it? I do not know. The only thing certain is that he never did.

With Domingo the foreman, it was another matter altogether. He too carried a gun. A big black man with a distant look in his eyes, he answered to no one but my grandfather in matters concerning the farm. His whole being was muscle hardened to stone by a difficult, long life in the country. He lived alone until two years before his death when he married a woman who, it is said, drove him to the grave. Off hours he did not say much and did not associate with the other hands. When he laughed, though, you could hear his cackle a half-league away.

For some reason I never understood, we became friends. We had nothing in common: he was a poor, black, middle-aged man from the country; I was a middle-class white boy from the city — shy, insecure, and always asking stupid questions that a diapered babe would have known the answer to. Sometimes he would invite me to his *bohío* for dinner. He'd kill a hen, have me clean it, and he'd make a stew, which we would eat right out of the pot with our hands and wash down with well water. He ate ravenously. While I had my two pieces of chicken and a few potatoes, he gulped down the rest of the pot and wiped it clean with pieces of bread.

He taught me how to make a trap for catching *chipojos* (large chameleons found in cow pastures), which wild birds were good eating and which were not, and how to shoe a horse. He often spoke of women. "Never trust them, but always treat them as if you do," he would say in a voice that sounded as if his nose were full of gravel.

The men didn't respect Domingo so much as fear him. They would mimic his voice and mannerisms behind his back but humbled themselves before him. They knew they were dealing with a man capable of anything. He was, after all, one of them. And he had a gun.

Domingo's one passion in life was cockfighting. Saturday nights after washing he would go into town for the cockfights, and maybe a woman, and come back the next morning. One Sunday morning he failed to return, nor did he appear on Monday. His wife finally sent someone to look for him. Domingo was found in the morgue. He had died of a heart attack in the ring after winning a substantial amount of money. His pockets had been picked clean and so no identification was found on him. Needless to say, the thief was never apprehended, and the wife never saw any of the money.

Beneath Domingo in the hierarchy of La Luisa were the year-round workers who lived with their families in the *batey*. The *batey,* across the highway from the farmhouse, was a cluster of thatched houses in the center of whch was an open area where people would often gather to dance and sing. The word itself is of Taíno Indian origin and means a tribal gathering place. These men did not, for the most part, cut cane, but rather ran the heavy machinery in the place. They drove the trucks and the one tractor and operated the loading crane and the weighing station. In addition, they each had specialties they performed after the *zafra*, or harvest, was over. Cuchito, for example, was the pig butcher;

Tito, the horse breaker; Alejandro, with a smile as wide as a river, was the expert mechanic; Neno, Tito's brother, held the dubious distinction of being the chief castrator. He emasculated everything from roosters to bulls.

Below the regular workers were the itinerant *macheteros.* They came during the *zafra* and lived in *barracones,* long buildings similar to barracks but with hammocks instead of beds. Within this group, status was determined not only by strength and the ability to cut the most cane but also by the machete one owned. The owner of an American-made machete had something over the owner of a Cuban one; best of all was owning a Collins, innately sharp and well balanced, the blade forged from a steel alloy that did not burnish.

The lowest level of the working force was occupied by the *guataqueros,* the hoers. Hoeing required the least amount of skill; almost anyone could do it and almost anyone did. *Guataqueros* were considered lazy, unreliable parasites, more likely than not to split your head open with the hoe for a quarter when your back was turned. *They never bathe. They drink turpentine. They sleep with pigs.* Lonely, crazed men, they were the lepers of La Luisa.

Life in La Luisa was probably little different from life in other *colonias.* If the *colono* was a benevolent, feudal ruler, he also tended to be well-off economically and live apart from the workers. Outside work, there was little, if any, contact between the farmer and the hands and their families. Even though my grandfather always made sure that no one in the *batey* went hungry, poverty was nonetheless ubiquitous. The *bohíos* had dirt floors and the children often went naked. Sanitary conditions were, at least as I remember them, very poor, with no plumbing or running water or toilets in the houses. Ignorance of even the simplest medical procedures made disease and death commonplace. This became clear to me one morning when a sad-faced man came to tell Fiquito that his son Raúl (a boy I had more than once played with) had died of dysentery overnight. In his frustration, Fiquito raged at the man, asking him why no one had come to him for help. He had the medicine. "It did not occur to us," was all the broken father could say.

Isolated, primitive, feudal La Luisa was destined for sudden death. The old government that had tolerated the system of the *colonias* fell, and a new one took its place. La Luisa was expropriated and taken over by the bureaucracy. The old house, which had stood in that spot since the days of Spanish rule, was torn down. In its place, I hear, a police interrogation center has been built.

At the general store in La Luisa. *Standing from left:* my Uncle Jaime; Maceira, the store owner; Grandfather Fiquito; Sergio Cartaya, Sr.; Domingo, the foreman; and my father; seated is my cousin Freddie (1944).

Zapata

MOSTLY WE DROVE through the swamp on our way to the Bay of Pigs, where the fishing was the best to be found anywhere on the island. The one road through went straight, with hardly a curve, into Playa Girón, which was to be the site of the ill-fated exile invasion in 1961. The sun was already setting when the first line was cast and it was only after the first light of dawn had tinted the eastern edge of the sky that we returned, laden with fish and ready to sleep through the morning.

From the car window, Zapata Swamp appeared as an endless expanse of brackish water and mangrove with an occasional *carbonero*'s shack. At times, columns of smoke in the distance rose toward the sky from, one imagined for they were never seen outright, slow burning coal ovens.

It happened that on a summer's day when I was eight years old and things were slow at the farm (the cane wasn't harvested until January), my mother's cousin Berto took a group of us crabbing in the swamp. We reached Zapata before dusk and stopped the jeep by a dirt road. To the right was a cow pasture; to the left, water as far as the eye could see — an inland shallow sea. Each of us, except my uncle Jaime, who carried a lantern, was handed a burlap sack and a hook fashioned out of a clothes hanger. The boys (myself and two cousins) were told to stay close to Jaime. As the sun went down, the crabs started creeping onto the road, at first only a few, then as it got darker, more and more came until the road was literally covered with them. They were ochre colored, about a foot long each, with claws as big as my hand, and they made eerie clacking and rasping noises as they crawled over each other. It was my first time crabbing and I was terrified, frozen in place by the morbid sensation that I could, at any time these creatures so wished, be devoured alive.

Everyone else was busy hooking the monsters by the large claw and dropping them into the sacks. This had to be done quickly, so as not to allow the crab to latch on to the hand holding the sack. "Those claws can really mangle a thumb," Berto had warned me with a cackle. Soon all the sacks but mine were filled and more were brought out. Jaime suggested we go into the cow pasture where we would find the females with their egg sacks bursting. To do this we had to crawl under a barbed-wire fence, the last strand of which lay dangerously close to the ground. Berto, his brother Raelo, Jaime, and my two cousins made it through easily, but as I slid under, I felt something hard under me. Thinking it was a crab (it was, most probably, a rock), I jerked up, slashing my back on one of the barbs. Within a minute or two my shirt was soaked with blood, and surrounding me was a cloud of mosquitoes as thick as coal smoke. I could barely see, I could barely breathe; I could not talk or even cry because I didn't want to swallow a mouthful of insects. My uncle took me back to the jeep, rolled up the windows, and told me to wait.

It was a hot night, as hot as it can get in the interior of Cuba. The inside of the jeep felt like a slow-burning oven. I was wet with my own blood; I was tired, alone, afraid, constantly watching the darkness outside, horrified that one of the *carboneros,* people who were said to practice the lowest of aberrations, from pederasty to infanticide, would show up. I waited in that metal coffin in such darkness I could not even see my hand in front of my face. I tried rolling the window down a crack to get some fresh air as the ferrous smell of my blood was making me nauseous, but within minutes a few mosquitoes had snuck in. Unable to see anything, I sat helplessly and listened to them buzzing round my ears until I could not bear it any longer. I leaned forward on the seat and waited for one of the little suckers to bite my bloody back. When I felt the prick, I threw myself backward hoping it would be too drunk with pleasure to escape. I don't know how many of the mosquitoes I crushed into oblivion; my strategy, however, kept me from going insane. It took me twenty years to recognize the value of that exercise. No matter how helpless the situation might really be, one's sense of helplessness will only be increased by inactivity. Few house fires will be put out with a garden hose, but the mere attempt will save one from the vise of despair.

The rest of the group showed up an eternity later with more crabs. The sacks were tied to the sides and top of the jeep, and we were ready for home. I felt the tension in every organ seep away in a long sigh of relief: bath, sleep, bath, sleep. But when Berto turned the key, nothing happened; the motor gave not even a whimper. The battery was dead. Now there were six of us inside the car sweating, cursing, and the crabs all around clacking and rasping.

Sometime after midnight we saw lights coming toward us in the distance. A truck full of soldiers with their Thompson machine guns and M-1's dangling limply over the sides pulled up next to us. A flashlight looked us over and fixed on Berto's face. He covered his eyes with his hand as if making a halfhearted salute. For a moment, there was absolute silence inside the cab — even the crabs stopped moving.

During the last years of the Batista dictatorship, groups of soldiers and police acting on their own (but with tacit official approval) roamed the interior in search of suspected sympathizers of the revolution. Of these groups, the most notorious was one led by a man named Masferrer. They called themselves Los Tigres de Masferrer. I had heard stories of how they ripped open the wombs of pregnant women and tied naked men on the ground, close to a mound of red ants, after spreading molasses on their groins. I had seen Los tigres photographed in *Bohemia,* a Cuban magazine, holding skulls of men and women they had supposedly tortured and killed. I was repulsed and, at the same time, fascinated by their sometimes ingenious methods. Their irrepressible brutality appealed to that part of me that sprinkled salt on toads and dropped live chameleons in jars of alcohol. This night, however, there was no fascination, only unadulterated trepidation.

Eventually, Berto got out and walked over to the truck's passenger seat. A low, barely audible murmur increased to loud talk and then open, if somewhat forced, laughter on Berto's part. A few minutes later he returned. "It's Captain Medeiros. He'll tow us to Jagüey." In the town the good captain woke up a mechanic who jump-started the jeep. Berto gave the mechanic a sack of crabs. He did not give the captain anything, not then.

We arrived at La Luisa in the early morning hours and we found Mina waiting up. When she saw me, miserably dirty and pale, her face opened like the dawn that was just beginning to spread over the *ceibas* in the back of the house, and she smiled. She took off my shirt, washed and disinfected my back, and prepared some *café con leche* and a couple of slices of warm bread with homemade butter. That was the most delicious bread I have ever tasted.

Tomás

MORE OFTEN THAN not, Tomás waited for me by the side of the road when I went out in the mornings. If I wasn't going to the fields with Fiquito, he would climb on the back of the horse, and off we went on our adventures. We always brought a frying pan and some lard, and perhaps some sweet potatoes Mina had cooked for us. If hunger struck, we'd shoot a half dozen mourning doves, clean them, and cook them in an open fire. To finish off the meal, we'd have fruit, — zapote, mamoncillo, mamey, caimito, whatever grew wild where we were — and then we'd rest under the shade of a tree.

Tomás was older than I by about three years — wild, untutored, and totally free from manners or morals. There was an inner goodness in him, however, and a simplicity that I have never seen in anyone else, except for perhaps Mamamía, but she is another story. His parents lived in the *batey,* but I do not remember who they were, and I do not think it mattered much to Tomás either. Once they were old enough to get around, children were pretty much left to their own devices in the *batey,* and they were taken care of by whoever happened to be around, that is, of course, until they were old enough to work. Just like all the other boys there, Tomás wore a ragged uniform: a sleeveless shirt without buttons; a pair of what now would be labeled cutoff shorts, but were nothing more than long pants so worn that they ended in strips at the knee; no shoes.

Tomás was a black Huck Finn to my Tom Sawyer. Boundlessly energetic and forever in search of adventure or mischief—life, not school, was his teacher. Whenever he was tired and in need of rest, he stopped and lay down; nothing would move him until he was refreshed. He knew where to find drinking water, which water holes drew ducks, when to go into the old slave cemetery so as not to disturb the spirits, and even which leaves to wipe with after going to the bathroom. "You use the guao leaf," he said, "and your ass will be itching for a week."

He liked to talk of owning a machete some day and going from farm to farm during the *zafra,* making money, traveling. And he liked to talk of spirits too. According to him, there was an evil spirit under every stone, a witch behind every tree. If you killed something on Good Friday, you would die the same way. He claimed he knew of someone in Pumariega (a nearby farm) who had stepped on a cockroach on that day and almost a year later had been run over by a locomotive. If you plucked a peacock in daylight, your hair would fall out. The best way to undo the curse of the evil eye was to hang the eye of a bull (an ox would not do) over your bed overnight; and to have a woman want you, you should buy stallion powder from a *santera* and stir it in the woman's coffee. When I asked, Tomás explained that stallion powder was dried and ground stallion testicles flavored with saffron to soften the taste. "Is stallion powder expensive?" I asked.

"A hundred dollars."

"A hundred dollars?"

"Yes, and the *santera* might ask you to go to bed with her. And they are ugly and dirty and they have mange on their teats."

"What do you do then?"

"Nothing. You have to do what a *santera* says. Otherwise she might put a curse on you like have your prick fall off. The only solution is to rub your thing ahead of time with sugarcane leaves until it is red and swollen. Then when she sees you like that, itching like crazy, she'll think you have the clap and let you go."

"I would never do that," I said.

"That depends on how much you want the girl."

In the end, no matter what we talked about, we would always

end up on the subject of sex. It was Tomás' obsession and was also becoming mine. Once, when passing a group of heifers my grandfather had just bought, he said, "Oh, I'd like to be a bull right now."

Another time, after we had been out all day, Tomás convinced me to chase down a ewe because he said he was horny as hell. He got off the horse and told me to drive the ewe away from the herd. I did as he said, but the ewe was no easy catch. After an hour of pursuit, we changed tactics. Rather than chasing her out in the open, Tomás would hide behind a knoll and I would lead her to him. By this time the ram was snorting and hoofing the ground, but there was nothing he could do. I was between him and the ewe, and rams don't charge horses, or so I'd been told.

The strategy worked! Just as the ewe was cantering by the knoll Tomás leaped, his rags flailing in the air, and they both tumbled over. I dismounted and grabbed hold of the sheep, who was by now resigned through exhaustion to the worst of fates. Tomás sat up on the ground, head between his knees, wheezing and puffing.

"Well?" I asked.

"I can't," he said between breaths, "I'm too tired. You do it."

Suddenly, all of my urban, middle-class repressions and taboos grabbed hold of my stomach and made it twist with fear and disgust. Give me a girl, any girl, and I'll give it a shot. But a sheep? I couldn't summon up a single fantasy that would save the moment from being a total waste of time. "I don't feel like it," I heard myself say, and with that, I let go of the first female I ever held with designs other than receiving motherly or sisterly affection. May Zeus, Patron of Bestiality, forgive me!

It would be easy from a distance, especially from the perspective afforded us by a puritanical society, where middle-class morality reigns, to apply some psychological label to Tomás and, by so doing, judge him. But Tomás was not unusual. In Cuba, sexuality (not necessarily promiscuity) was a more prevalent force than it is in American society. Apart from any inequalities that prevailed between the sexes (and which, I believe, still exist, notwithstanding the present government's claims to the contrary), Cubans, certainly the ones I grew up with, recognized a difference between man and woman, a difference that manifested itself primarily and overwhelmingly through one's sexuality. It was only after the acceptance of such a difference that members of the opposite sex would deal with each other both socially and professionally. This was the case in middle-class society of Havana. In the country, in the quasi-tribal life of the *batey,* where life was ordained by nature, sex was of primary importance, and for a boy entering manhood like Tomás, there was little else.

That same summer, after an especially heavy rain, I was as usual going out in the morning and I saw Tomás waving at me and jumping like a mad man. When I reached him, he told me that the Hondón, a low-lying cow pasture, was flooded and that all the kids were already there swimming. It so happened that among them there was a girl, a mulatta with a nice, well-developed body and eyes as green as sugarcane, that Tomás had been interested in all summer. When we entered the pasture, Tomás jumped off the horse and raced over to the girl. (I forget her name but I remember her skin, the color of raw sugar, and again her eyes as if I had seen her yesterday.) I dismounted, tied the horse to a fence post, and took my clothes off, keeping my underpants on. In the heat of passion Tomás had not bothered to disrobe (I should say disrag). When I turned to where the group was mulling about, I saw a scene right out of Greek mythology. Here was this wondrously beautiful girl running away, with Tomás trailing and lifting up her skirt, his coal black penis straight up in the air. She kept saying, "No, Tomás, no," laughing, turning this way and that, trying to pull her skirt down while Tomás thrust wildly at the air. No doubt, had a fly crossed his path it would have been skewered. I do not recall if Tomás satisfied his lust for the girl then or at any other time; the one thing I know is that they were having the time of their lives, and so was I.

The following summer something happened that put a sudden end to our friendship. My sister and I were riding through the *batey* when Tomás appeared suddenly out of nowhere and grabbed my sister by the ankle. "I want to screw you," he said staring up and smiling. I exploded with rage, kicked Tomás out of the way, and galloped to the house. My grandmother sat on the porch, and my sister, crying, told her what Tomás had said. "Put the horse away," was the only response Mina gave. After this, I hardly saw

Tomás and, when we did meet, he seemed distant and withdrawn, almost afraid. It wasn't until a few years later, already in exile, that my mother told me how Tomás had been dealt with.

On hearing of the matter, Fiquito told Domingo to "have a word with that boy." Domingo, in turn, took the boy to the *arboleda,* tied him to a tree, and shot his gun at the ground between the boy's legs. "The next time you do anything like that," he is said to have warned, "I'll shoot your balls off."

Both my sister and I had forgotten the matter that same evening and doubtless Tomás had too. But not the adults. I have several dark spots in my memory, and this is one of them, for I have never really understood how they — Domingo and my grandparents, but especially my grandparents — could ever have dealt so harshly and unfairly with a boy, a boy who happened to be my friend. But, as I said before, La Luisa was a primitive place.

Pig Slaughter

ONCE FIQUITO PICKED the hog, Cuchito was sent for. He brought a long, thin knife with a sharp point wrapped in a piece of burlap. The pig, tied to the *anón* tree in the center of the yard, squealed and tried to pull itself free. My grandfather asked me to untie the animal and bring it to a stone slab by the kitchen, a sort of porcine sacrificial altar. I pulled and pulled, but the hog was stronger than I. Fiquito yelled to pull harder, not to be so gentle. I yanked as hard as I could and the pig stumbled over a rock and fell sideways with its head tucked under its chest. It lay in that position until another yank forced him up.

By the stone, Cuchito flipped the animal on its side and kneeled over it. It was squealing again — a high-pitched swan song that came and went as its breath gave out — death siren, lard rattle — its back legs kicking in search of a hold, finding only air and pebbles scratching its thigh. Cuchito-executioner raised the hog's right forefoot with his left hand and felt with his thumb for a spot where he knew the blade would do its cold, lethal duty. Quickly, before the pig squirmed free of his grasp, he reached for the knife that was stuck handle up on the ground about a foot from the animal's throat and struck.

All I could see was a flash entering the chest and a spurt of blood, thick red, shooting sideways onto the ground and gathering into a deepening puddle. The pig squealed even higher now in one continuous note — no use stopping to breathe, life leaving in a blinding and deafening fountain of noise and color — followed by gurgling and choking as the blood reached the throat, stained teeth and snout, and dribbled out the nostrils and mouth. By this time, the squealing had turned to grunts and the pig, more carcass than animal, convulsed, eyes glazed slits through which no light could enter, but a slow darkness, like a tide filling the spaces life had vacated. A stretch of the back legs caused one final bowel movement and the feces came to rest on a soft, olive mound under that part of it soon to be smoked ham.

When Fiquito was certain that death, not life, coursed through the pig's veins, he motioned to Cuchito to carry the carcass over to the scrubbing table where they poured boiling water over it and, with a piece of soapstone, scrubbed it clean of hair. Cuchito again took to the knife, drove the point carefully in the throat and, with the concentration of a surgeon, sliced through skin and lard, the knife following the contours of the rib cage to the edge, where it dipped into the soft flab of the belly all the way to the anal sphincter that, cut, spewed forth more of the olive waste. With a dull machete and a hammer, he cracked the rib cage and the jaw. He discarded the tools carelessly on the ground, grabbed each side of the crevice, hands deep in the hold, and pulled until the ribs let go of the spine and the chest cavity opened like a pulpy fruit exposing a chaos of purple organs and blue and yellow intestines. And then I wondered if I were split so unceremoniously like that whether my organs too would shine amorphously in the sun like multicolored gelatin.

One sweeping cut inside the chest cavity freed the guts and they spilled into a bucket placed at the lower end of the table. More than spilled, they slithered like oyster meat into a galvanized throat. Cuchito asked Fiquito if doña Mina wanted the *mondongo*. "Not this time," he answered, after which Cuchito proceeded to cut the carcass into pieces: hams, ribs, chops, until slowly the shape of the pig disappeared and all that was left was the head with the spine still attached. This he hung on a hook on the outer wall of the tack room. It was his pay for the job. His woman would make spine soup tonight.

We took the guts, Cuchito and I, to the *arboleda,* the grove of

La Luisa from behind, facing the kitchen. Just to the left around the corner, was the site of the pig slaughter. Workmen came to the window for Mina's coffee (1937).

trees that grew behind the outbuildings, and dumped them under a giant mimosa for the vultures to take care of.

Later, when I was busy with something else, I glanced up and saw the figure of Cuchito, the head and spine slung over his shoulder, walking lightly away over the red ground.

Romana

THE STORM APPEARED on the northern horizon far enough away so that it didn't much worry me. I figured I had at least an hour to get home. In ten minutes, the clouds were directly overhead. Heavy drops of rain pummeled my head and lightning struck all around me on the bare field. I had to get under cover quickly. I whipped the horse and off we went, flying through the rain toward the *batey,* thunder muffling all sound but the stinging water's whoosh. When I reached the *romana,* every inch of me was wet and I was panting harder than the horse, from fear or hard riding, I don't know which. Alejandro and another man I did not know were there, waiting for the front to pass.

They were talking of the weather and how dangerous it was to be out in lightning as thick as the rain, and I remembered my mother's cousin Lando, who had been struck by lightning while riding through a field during a squall just like today's and had been burned to a crisp, fried with his boots on. But I had survived: I had made it through the watery nightmare and guided my horse to safe ground.

There happened to be a car parked inside the weighing station and, in order to get closer to the men, I sat on the front fender. Soon my legs were swinging back and forth to the rhythm of their talk, slow and easy and melodious, the talk of people in tune with the caprices of Nature.

As my legs on their downward trajectory bumped the bottom of the fender, I felt something grab my pant cuff and tug violently at it. At first, I thought my pants had gotten caught on a piece of car metal and I yanked up as hard as I could. Fixed on my leg, squirming and growling like the devil himself, was the creature, a weasel. Panic hit me like a lightning bolt. I fell on the ground rolling and twisting, all the while trying to kick the beast away. The men hovered over me until one of them broke free of the initial surprise and, realizing what was happening, grabbed the animal by the tail. But the weasel would not let go; the jaws were clamped for good. Then, whoever it was that had a hold on it (I can't remember if it was the stranger or Alejandro) swung a machete's handle down on the weasel's head several times until it was no longer a head but a messy pulp of bone and tissue and brain matter. As the jaws were still shut, they had to cut the pants away from me, then asked in a guarded tone if it had bitten me. "I don't know," I answered in a daze, wiping sweat and dust from my face. They checked my ankle and calf, but there was not a scratch. "Boy, you are lucky," said Alejandro. "That bastard was rabid."

El Guayabal

ACROSS THE WAY from the farmhouse, out behind the *barra-cones*, was a grove of guava trees enclosed in part by a stone wall and, where the wall had crumbled away, by barbed wire and bushes. Here Fiquito kept his pigs, fifty or sixty semiwild, scrawny creatures that fed on the fruit that dropped from the trees. Adjoining the entrance gate on either side were the ruins of slave quarters. What walls remained were cracked and crumbly, eaten away by time and weather, and here and there were mounds of rocks covered by weeds.

Besides pigs, ghosts lived here. And it was the latter I came for: women in long skirts with handkerchiefs tied around their heads; naked children playing *quimbumbia,* a stick game resembling baseball; the men returning from the fields in chains, their skins glazed with sweat; even Justo, the ex-slave who walked up and down the highway sneering at children and cursing at cars — Satan's chariots he called them — I saw him as a boy like me, already working at whatever chores were assigned young slaves; in short, I peopled the Guayabal with the ancestors of the people of La Luisa, except their faces were the faces of Alejandro and Cuchito and Tomás and Caridad, the maid.

It dawned on me that the lives of these people had not changed much. They wore no leg irons, they weren't shipped or bought or sold, but the *freedom* accorded them by emancipation had been a dim promise, always just beyond the horizon. Their reality was total subjugation to work and the struggle for survival. How was this different from anyone else's situation? Every adult I knew worked and struggled and slaved. But there was a difference between the people of La Luisa and members of my family that eluded me at the time, and it took the experience of emigration and exile, threatening as it did our sense of security, to come to terms with that difference, to accept it in the mind, in the heart, and in the body.

I was a twelve-year-old member of a middle-class family and, as such, took for granted the most basic of freedoms — freedom from hunger, from disease, from ignorance — that were still beyond the grasp of many of the people of La Luisa. An empty stomach, a sick body, and an uneducated mind cannot entertain any thoughts other than to be full, healthy, and knowing. Those other freedoms — freedom of speech, of movement, of ownership — that the Cuban middle class held so dear and involved them in decades of political struggle were luxuries, really, and in a society such as Cuba, they were precarious at best. Many of the people I grew up with — family and friends — had worked very hard to achieve and maintain these, but most lost them practically overnight. They were left with a one-way ticket out of the society or into jail.

It was a particularly hot day when, in search of cool shade, I went deeper into the grove than I had ever been before and discovered a small clearing. In the middle were the remains of an *ingenio,* an old sugar mill, the huge grinding stone still standing vertically on the base as if it had stopped working only yesterday. I had never encountered anything like this in La Luisa. This was to be my private place, my link to the past, the monolith of history I would return to time and again to think, to fantasize, to be myself, to be someone other than myself.

Whiling away afternoons in the clearing, I was to observe how light changed the appearance of the stone. On overcast days it was gray and showed its age, with every nick and crack on its surface clearly delineated. When the sun hit it directly, though, it shone so brightly that it appeared to spew its own golden light — a round sponge that sucked up sun and radiated with it.

Once I stayed later than usual and, as the sun set, the color changed rapidly from its usual vibrant gold to ochre to pink, not the pastel hue of flowers but an intense color that threatened to turn red at the blink of an eye. The change was so violent and quick that it scared me. My heart wanted to burst through my chest and my ears hurt. A phenomenon beyond my understanding was unfolding before me faster than I could account for it. But I did not leave right away. My eyes were fixed unblinking on the round stone with the square hole in its center; my palms were sweaty, my knees weak. Somewhere from deep inside me came the recognition that I had seen that almost red before, been enveloped, drawn sustenance and warmth from it, and I trembled, caught between fear and a longing to curl up and sleep.

A few weeks later, deep in August, I returned to the clearing determined to move the millstone. I pushed and shoved it from all directions, but it would not budge. Frustration led to anger, anger to hardheadedness. I left and came back with my horse, Maltrote, and a heavy rope. I tied the rope through the stone's hole and onto the saddle horn, then whipped the horse. The rope grew taut, the horse's hooves clopped heavily on the pebbly ground until I saw the thing budge a few inches. *That wasn't too difficult,* I thought. *That's enough. The stone still has life.* But it was too late. The horse was still pulling and the stone, slowly moving in the direction of the pull, toppled off its base and cracked into several pieces on the ground.

I never went back to the clearing, but I have often wondered if the millstone's rubble is still there, if the Guayabal is there, or whether it's all been cleared to make room for more cane fields, or yet more cells where suspects waiting to be interrogated are housed, less free and with less hope than the slaves I dreamed about.

Mina

I KNOW LITTLE of my grandmother's childhood. I never bothered to ask her about it, and now that she is old and I am interested, I do not dare. Memories have a way of hiding in the closet of consciousness. To have an old person open that closet door, especially someone as close to death as Mina, can be an unsettling experience, laden with sorrow and remorse.

Not that she had much of a childhood: she married Fiquito when she was fourteen. The marriage caused quite a stir, not because of her age or the fact that my grandfather was twelve years her senior, but rather because their mothers were sisters. Whatever objections were raised to the union, I imagine, came not so much from Mina's side of the family as from Fiquito's. Mina's mother had married a man of rather modest means whose life had been one continuous struggle against bad fortune, while her sister, older and perhaps more calculating, married a wealthy man of the area. Ignacio González owned several food warehouses, a sawmill, real estate in Pedro Betancourt and was, in addition, the administrator of don Pedro Arenal's vast landholdings, of which La Luisa and Jardines were once part. Thus, it could not have been difficult for Mina's parents to look the other way when the matter first came up.

The Gonzálezes might have raised their eyebrows and worried; they might even have mentioned their doubts to Fiquito, but I do not believe that what his parents thought mattered much to him. He was, after all, twenty-six years old, independent, and headstrong. The fifth oldest of ten children, my grandfather was the most responsible and the hardest worker, traits that must have endeared him to his father. Such a model son had to be allowed the freedom to make his own decision, especially since Mina was, from all they could gather, a good, quiet girl, knowledgeable in the arts of homemaking, and sure to bear Fiquito strong, healthy children. And if all this was not enough, it was obvious that the two were very much in love. With the blessings of their respective families on one hand and the proper dispensation from church authorities on the other, my grandparents became husband and wife.

They first moved into a *bohío* Ignacio had especially built for them, not far from the main house in La Luisa. A year later, when my grandmother was all of fifteen years old, their first child, my aunt Minita, was born. And here began, so my grandmother asserts, an idyllic marriage. There were always flowers in the backyard, she tells me, and in my imaginings, fueled by traditional Cuban country songs, there were butterflies too, yellow and black and orange, and potted plants hanging from the palm-bark walls, and in the center of their garden — for this was so in most of the *bohíos* I had seen in my wanderings — a well with a crank spigot must have stood. No doubt there was no bathroom but an outhouse, far enough away from the house to make its existence inconspicuous, and boot scrapers by the two doors. Whatever pictures hung on the wall inside must have been cut out of calendars and framed cheaply, if at all. Among the few they had, I'm sure, was a print of Jesus and his sacred heart displayed prominently in the small living room.

I imagine, too, that the *bohío* became cramped with the arrival of the second daughter, Julieta, and that my grandfather asked his father for the main house, now that Ignacio spent most of his time in town. The father must have been pleased, for it was a boon to have a son who, unlike him, was more than willing to live in the country and take over the running of the farm, which Ignacio, old and rheumatic, felt to be more and more a burden.

Fiquito and Mina were coming up in the world and she was faced with having to learn to administer a large household with maids, cleaning ladies, cooks, a charcoal bin as large as one of the bedrooms in her previous house, and two other daughters that came in swift succession. La Luisa, Mina explained to me, was quite a change. It took her awhile to adjust.

Adjust she did, however, the transition eased by the jump in status, by the larger house, and by the eventual purchase of a home in town, the ultimate symbol of affluence for a *colono's* family.

In the case of Mina and Fiquito, the need to have access to society was made even more pressing by the fact that they had four daughters to marry off. Few suitable prospects would be found in the country, and if Pedro Betancourt was hardly the center of the civilized world, the town did have its sprinkling of professionals — doctors, lawyers, merchants — as well as the other *colonos* who had bought into the town for much the same reason as my grandparents. As with any urban center no matter how small, Pedro Betancourt provided the social institutions where young people of proper family and economic backgrounds could interact. There was the Liceo, an exclusive quasi-political club that held parties and dances; two movie houses, one of which played American movies exclusively; the church, with the plaza in front, which people frequented on Sundays; and above all, there were the houses themselves with their wide front porches, which allowed the girls to entertain suitors under the watchful eyes of the mothers.

The townhouse was a boon to Mina in that it broke the isolation and loneliness of life in the country. *Colonias* were far away from each other and social visits were at best occasional. While their husbands worked ten or twelve hours a day, six days a week, the women were deprived of contact with women other than domestic help. In town, a visit required crossing the street or leaning on the veranda that divided one porch from another. The one thing that kept women like Mina from buckling under the pressure of keeping two houses was the frequent and spontaneous social contact that was part of town life and that, in the case of Mina, she had never really experienced, even as a child.

It was through these casual meetings that the business of the town, mostly in the form of gossip, was relayed. News of troubled marriages, deflowered maidens, shotgun weddings, drunkenness, and gambling spread like fire from porch to porch. Once the men arrived from work, however, gossip toned down and less interesting but no less important matters, such as weddings, illnesses, high school graduations, first communions, and the like, were discussed.

If I was privy to the women's more open banter, it was because of my age, which made it appear as if I was not aware enough to be interested. But listen I did, and with great concentration. I loved the gossip and the lighthearted banter of these women. Their laughter was often sarcastic, but rarely vicious — as if they understood too well the plights they described, for everyone had been young once, everyone had seen trouble — and I too would be infected, laughing at poor so and so who was caught by her mother kneading her beau's *chorizo;* or at the old widow who hung up negligees several sizes too small to dry on the line in hopes of inspiring the envy of her neighbors.

One of the women's favorite topics of conversation was the amorous antics of tío Rañón. Rañón, a Spaniard by birth, was married to my great-aunt Julita, who was as big and fat as he was small and thin. He owned a general store and was said to make a pass at any woman who entered the establishment alone. He kept feminine articles low, so that he could admire the women's buns as they bent over. "I have seen him stretching his neck over the counter like a hungry vulture as I was picking up a bottle of perfume," my mother's cousin Milda once said. "What shopkeeper in his right mind would keep perfume on the floor?" And he did not just look. A lady once left the store in a fume because Rañón had put his hand on her buttocks. When confronted by the irate husband, he defended himself by maintaining that he was only helping the lady keep her balance. That night he went home with a black eye.

The women also chuckled over Julita and Rañón in bed: he with his oversized bald head and a body that seemed to lose itself in the baggy clothes he wore; she, bountiful as two Renoir women put together. "He's had to learn to swim to keep from drowning in her." "His elevator shoes don't help him where it counts." "It takes him one week to finish with a part of her, then he starts on the next."

One day the women were talking as usual on the porch when all of a sudden there arose a scream from the group. I was sitting on the floor, flipping through a comic book I had read several times, when I saw my aunt Dinorah holding her breast and swooning in apparent pain. A bee had landed on it and, as she was trying to swat it away, had stung her right through the blouse close to the nipple. As the flustered females huddled around her, Rañón walked by on his way home for lunch. After inquiring as to the source of the trouble, he stated in his proud Spanish voice that he knew just what to do. Like a lap dog forgotten amidst the confusion, I tagged along after the whole group into my grandmother's bedroom. Rañón asked for a pair of tweezers and then helped Dinorah undo her blouse. When the breast finally appeared, Rañón held it, red and swollen as it was, and tried to pluck the stinger out with the tweezers. I noticed, though, that his eyes were fixed on the nipple, not on the sting. He was talking nervously, in short bursts, and there was a bit of a smile showing through his lips. Finally he said, "This won't do. I'll have to suck it out." When my grandmother heard this, she forgot all about her agonizing daughter and yelled, *"Sal de aquí, viejo sinvergüenza"* (Get out of here, you dirty old man). Rañón straightened and, screwing up his neck, responded, "Well, if I'm no longer needed, I think I'll be going."

It was the last anyone heard of the matter, for the following day Rañón and Mina were as civil and friendly to each other as they had ever been. My aunt Dinorah's breast returned to its normal size and color and has lived a long and healthy life.

Mina and Fiquito lived for others. Rare was the time when there weren't people in their houses — family, friends, even strangers passing through who happened to stray in at dinnertime. How they found time for intimacy, I don't know, for their bedroom was open at any hour of the day, and on nights when the evening sounds and shadows kept the grandchildren from sleep, we knew we could always find a haven in their bed. None of us, so far as we can remember, was ever turned away.

Her in-laws were right in their assessment: Mina turned out to be as good a wife as any man could ask for. She supported her husband, fed him, and kept his home and children in order. Most of all, she was absolutely faithful to him. I refer here not to sexual fidelity — it would never have entered her mind to commit adultery — but to her trust in him as a person and as a man, a trust, she maintains without a flicker of doubt in her voice, he returned in kind. Even now, twenty-nine years after his death, that faith still burns in her.

No doubt most people today would consider Mina an anachronism, would find her devotion to Fiquito repulsive and psychotic. After all, we of the latter half of the twentieth century consider independence from human ties the be-all and end-all of existence. And she has not made the transition to life in exile very well, but I can safely say that few Cubans have. We have worn masks and disguised ourselves to make it appear that we have barely missed a step from rhumba to rock-and-roll; regardless, all of us live in our past as we must. It is just that in Mina's case the past was so much fuller, so much more graced with love. She is quite ill and will die sooner than we want. When she does, the family will be that much closer to being set adrift in this cold, anonymous sea, where the only beacon is the self.

As I grow older and sink ever deeper into the loneliness of American society, this sense of family, of openness to others that she and others of the family have deeded to me, becomes increasingly dear. Because I dread isolation, because I have been taught to define myself through others, I fight that tendency of our society to shut the door on anyone who is not a card-carrying member of the nuclear family. Above all, I am terrified of growing old alone, discarded in an old-age home because my children will be too busy to care for me or because my presence makes them feel uncomfortable, put-upon, and limited from pursuing that vacuous activity called self-realization.

But I digress. To say that Mina and Fiquito led an idyllic life is to fall into the trap memory must constantly be wary of. Troubles came to them as they come to everyone. Farming is an uncertain occupation, and the tensions of planting and harvesting ripple through the nerves of all who are involved with the earth. Add to this the fact that all my grandparents' children were women little interested in farming and you begin to realize that their lives were tinged with a particular kind of existential anguish. What would become of the land when they died? And who would carry on?

When Fiquito died, my grandmother refused ever to go back to La Luisa. She ran the place, with help from my uncle Jaime, from a distance. Without my grandfather there, the farm lost its magic for me as well. More and more, I preferred to spend vacations at the beach. My last summer in Cuba, I stayed only two weeks at the farm. Even the birds seemed boring.

The City

THE VILLAGE OF San Cristóbal de la Habana was first founded on the southern shore of the island in 1515. The area proved to be unhealthy to the settlers and so, in 1518, they moved north, first to the Almendares River, and from there, a few kilometers east, where they discovered a calm, well-protected bay. Tired of packing their village up and carting it in every direction, they dropped it down near the lower end of the bay. Good enough, they must have thought. Warm breeze, clean ocean, few mosquitoes — here we'll stay come hell or high water. Both came, the first in the form of pirates who pillaged and burned the city twice in a period of thirty-seven years before it occurred to the residents to fortify it with a wall and several forts placed strategically around the bay. The fortifications did not deter the pirates, who made many more sorties against the city, but it did keep Havana from ever being totally destroyed again. Later came the hurricanes, but no wall could keep those out and the city has always been subject to the ravages of tropical storms. The worst of the cyclones hit the city in 1926, during which fishing boats floated down streets like deserted gondolas, dead cows dropped on rooftops, and houses flew overhead like birds.

In this city, so much at the mercy of the whims of men and weather, I was born. The Havana of my childhood is the most beautiful city I have known: cosmopolitan yet small by comparison with most capitals, modern yet creaking with age, busy as cities are, but easy, and gentle on the nerves, full of the tropical sun and brilliant, but also shadowy and mysterious. Here I grew up, I learned to live, and I learned a little bit of death, too.

The one place I loved to go most on Sunday afternoons was the Malecón, a wide boulevard that rounded the bay from Almendares to the statue of Antonio Maceo, the hero of the War of Independence. The waves crashed against the quay that kept the sea from eating away at the pavement, sending huge explosions of spray over the wall and onto the sidewalk. Groups of boys played tag with the water, walking until a wave crashed, then running from the spray, sometimes right into the street and the oncoming traffic, to avoid getting drenched.

Across the street where only the mist reached, the boulevard was lined with stalls selling foods and drinks of all kinds: *fritas, papas rellenas, empanadas, pasteles, pan con lechón, guarapo,* papaya juice, mango juice, and the oranges peeled and cut the way you wanted. Up and down the sidewalk, *cafeteros* with their thermoses full of black, strong coffee intoned their cry: *Café, un kilo, un kilo café.* There were also *maniceros* carrying large tin cans loaded with peanut cones: *Maní, manicero aquí, cucuruchos de maní.*

At the intersections, photographers dressed in dark, wrinkled suits took pictures of whole families out for a Sunday stroll, which they developed in cans hanging under their tripods. And everywhere there were children playing, chasing each other, darting in and out through groups of passersby, daring each other to do this and that, the mothers chastising, threatening, the fathers walking imperturbably on in their white *guayaberas.*

On the horizon, the shipping lanes provided a parade of vessels that filled a boy's head with seafaring fantasies: cargo ships, fishing trawlers, sailing schooners, warships, and always the cruise ships that slowly made their way into the bay and spewed their cargo of *americanos* in for a week of leisure.

Once my father took me to the port to see a cruise ship come in. It was a crowded place. Stacks of crates lined the sides of buildings; some of them, from the looks of their weathered wood, had been there a long time. The fresher boxes, with lettering from far-off places like Spain, Germany, and China, were piled on the older ones. Closer to waterside, stevedores rushed by carting luggage or sacks of sugar. *Por ahí voy! Por ahí voy!* Trucks backed into warehouses, honking lest someone get in the way; small tractors pulled cartloads of imports, and the smell of diesel permeated the area.

Two long landing docks kept me from seeing the ship approach, but I did notice the long column of smoke from its chimney clouding the blue sky before dispersing into the atmosphere. After what seemed like an interminably long time, the black bow of the ship turned the corner. It surprised me that such a large ship could move so slowly until I realized that the ship was being pushed by towboats. Once the ship was parallel to the dock, long ropes were hurled to groups of men on shore who pulled the boat in and secured it. Out of nowhere, dozens of boys, some not much older than I, dove into the water and swam to the side of the ship. From there they yelled to the tourists, *moni, moni.* The tourists obliged by raining a shower of coins into the water. The boys disappeared into the brackish green water around the ship and came back up mumbling for more (they kept the coins in their mouths). The tourists looked down amazed, turning and calling to others out of view who came and gawked and laughed and threw more *moni* in as if they were feeding goldfish.

Once on shore, the Americans were greeted by a band playing *guarachas* and by waiters holding trays of daiquiris and Cuba Libres. Some danced, right there on the port; others drank and guffawed saying *Gracious, gracious, muchos gracious* to anyone who went by, waiter or not; others still looked suspiciously around as if they expected someone to attack them at any moment.

These tourists acted just like I expected Americans to act: raucous and open, dressed in conspicuous clothing that identified them immediately as vacationers, joyful on cue, and at the same time somewhat wary, as if they did not quite trust the fun they were having. Foreigners, in other words: creatures to be avoided unless you were selling them souvenirs or otherwise trying to take their *moni.* Little did I know that a few years later I was to be the foreigner in their land.

I was impressed by the beauty of American women — blonde, tall, with fair freckled skin and long shapely legs, just like movie stars. That afternoon when I came home, I sat and dreamed of them, of their ruby red lips and the curves of their calves accentuated by high-heeled shoes. While their men drank and smoked cigars, they danced with each other or with the singer of the band. Oh, to have been that singer!

If Havana was a playground for American tourists, it was one for me as well, although in a very different way. By the time I was eleven, I was allowed access to the whole city. Weekends, I would take a bus on my own and go to movies and later walk the Rampa or the Paseo del Prado, an old stately boulevard in the middle of which was a walk shaded by almond trees. Many people gathered there: street musicians, maids on their days off, policemen too tired to walk their beat, bootblacks, fruit vendors singing their wares, and the ever-present beggars.

On one of my weekend jaunts, I walked the whole length of the Paseo del Prado and, on my way back, I heard to my right a strange sound — someone coughing and gagging at the same time. Under a cornice of one of the government buildings was a legless man on a dolly. He was vomiting a glue-like substance into a jar, but its mouth was too narrow so that the ooze spilled over on his hands and long strings of it hung down from his jaw. The more he tried to aim into the jar, the more violent his spasms. I watched him as long as I could stand and then went over to him. If he noticed the look of horror on my face, he made no sign. Between breaths he lifted his eyes at me and said, *"Pañuelo,"* pointing to his back pocket with a glazed finger. I put my thumb and forefinger into the pocket and pulled out a wrinkled, gray handkerchief and handed it to him. It was all he wanted and all I could do for him. I walked on, never once looking back.

Such scenes were not uncommon in the city, and in this respect, Havana was much like any other Latin American city. There was great wealth there, and some areas had a Babylonian splendor that would have put the gaudiest Hollywood set to shame; yet, in the streets, tucked away in the shadows, often within spitting distance of a thirty-room mansion, lurked the forgotten: the crippled, the ill, the unlucky. No amount of tourist and sugar money would ever help them; no number of grandiose churches would save them.

Beggars were most visible around churches, particularly on Sundays, when they preyed on the guilt of the pious. Mostly they were ignored; sometimes a gratuitous coin was dropped in their

direction. Once, walking out of church with my great-grandmother, I saw a young priest kicking a blind man on the steps of
the church of Villanueva. Was he deranged? Did he think himself
Christ and the poor man a moneylender? I looked at my great-
grandmother, eager for some wise answer, some reassurance. Her
soft, ancient eyes answered me with a saddened, resigned look.
She went on clutching her missal. I followed her home.

For the most part, middle-class *habaneros* were indifferent to
the poverty around them. Life was easy and bountiful and time
passed slowly. Perhaps it was the weather — hot brilliant days
under blue skies mottled by cumulus clouds — or the sea, which
most of the time set a seductive rhythm few could resist. Even
children heard the sirens singing. The vibrant city floating on the
Caribbean gave up all pretense of social guilt and thrived on the
sea breeze. Puritanical and progressive were adjectives no one
would ever have thought of tacking on prerevolutionary Havana.
The poor could always look to the sea for solace, for there was no
help from those whom fortune had graced.

In such a setting, it was easy to let things go until another day.
Were the weather not enough, another factor, equally strong, kept
the *habaneros* from striving for social change and the betterment
of their unfortunate brothers. And that was blood. The Cuban
soul, particularly the Havanan soul, is a hybrid of the Spanish and
the African. Different as these two races are, they are fatalistic to
an extreme.

At the periphery of European civilization, shaken throughout
history by political and social cataclysms, the Spaniards adopted
fatalism from the Moors, cloaked themselves and their social institutions with it, and survived within an ever more resilient, if
brittle, self. The Africans, however, were forever overwhelmed by
a geography and climate beyond control and understanding. Less
European, less self-obsessed, the Africans survived within the
tribe. Beyond it was darkness and death forever stalking. It was
resignation to the forces of Nature and a parallel affirmation of
the insignificance of an individual before ruthless Fate that kept
the Africans from being devoured by fear and hopelessness.

The *habaneros* sprang from these two sources. Except for the
occasional hurricane, nature did not brutalize them, and, by the

mid 1950s, they were two generations away from the centuries-old grip of monarchy. What repression they experienced was the making of their own political uncertainty and indifference. More-over, the incompetence and corruption of the dictatorships that followed one another since independence were not particularly oppressive. Only those who stood in the way of the rulers' self-enrichment suffered. For the most part, the middle-class *haba-neros* prospered with a minimum of effort. Their inherited fa-talism allowed them the luxury to feel little compassion for those around them or guilt about their own well-being. Changing the political system would do no good. The law in Cuba was little more than a joke, easier to skirt than to follow, and those who obeyed it were considered more naïve than moral. In this sense, Cubans were, and still are to some extent, light years away from their North American neighbors.

Whatever political and social activism existed came from two small but rather influential groups: workers and university stu-dents. By banding together, workers were able to exert great po-litical pressure. Labor laws were instituted that assured a mini-mum wage, worker's compensation, retirement pensions, and other benefits. Cuban workers, like their counterparts in other countries of the world, were a pragmatic bunch: they wanted to improve their lot. Thus socialism appealed to them (traditional communism in Cuba was strongest among unions) insofar as it offered a system that professed quite specifically the apotheosis of the worker.

University students reacted against dictatorship and corrup-tion in more ideological ways, at least initially. Younger and bet-ter educated as a whole, they embraced political philosophies with evangelical fervor. Paradoxically, this same zeal led student activists to become quite violent, not only against whatever gov-ernment ruled at the time but also against themselves. By the late 1940s and early 1950s, student political groups reached their zenith. But the violence that had become their trademark and the power that these groups gained, both within and without the university, were such that student activism degenerated into a struggle for control of the alma mater and of the political process itself. Ideology became a mask to be worn when necessary. Power was the real goal. It was in this milieu that Fidel Castro, and many of those who have at one point or another surrounded him, developed as a leader.

I did not know any of this when growing up. Nevertheless I was, as were most children in Havana, more politically aware than many children and some adults in the United States. It took a great deal of effort to ignore politics in the Cuba of the 1950s. A group of young men and women, most of them from the ranks of the cynical middle class, were challenging the Batista government and were making significant inroads. The media pulsated with reports of strikes, demonstrations, and the latest incursions of the guerrilla forces in the mountains. As if this were not enough, there was always the threat of being caught in the midst of a demonstration or in the cross fire during a street battle, or of having the theater one was in blown up by a terrorist bomb. On more than one occasion, my parents came to pick me up in mid-movie after hearing rumors of a possible street disturbance or general strike.

All the revolutionary activity going on around me, however, never deterred me. Most of the time I came and went as I pleased (provided I had the bus fare) and thus I had the opportunity of discovering Havana, both its dark and light sides, without the cumbersome interference of adults. No one was there to turn my face away from poverty, or to divert my attention when a prostitute walked by, or to point at the sights and make inane adult remarks about them, or to admire for me the clear sunlight reflecting on the mansions of La Quinta Avenida.

It was Havana that made me love all cities. It is Havana to which I compare them and always find them lacking. I harken back to my boyhood with its images of streets, buildings, statues, parks, people, and the sky blue sea that caressed and brutalized them and wonder how the city of my birth has changed since I left, whether the stories of its decline are true — if I will ever return.

The Compound

WE LIVED IN a small, unpretentious three-bedroom house on 167th Street, a block away from La Quinta Avenida. My sister Silvia, aunt Dinorah, and I shared one bedroom, my parents occupied the master, and the maid and her husband the third, which was off the kitchen on the other side of the house. A front porch, garage, living and dining rooms, and a large back porch made up the rest of the house. Add the family bathroom and closet-size maid's bathroom and this accounted for our interior living space.

Next to us lived my aunt Chala, her husband, Gustavo, and my grandmother Juana María. Next to them, in a house identical to the other two, were my great-aunt Lolita, her husband, Pepe, and their son José Antonio. On La Quinta Avenida, which ran perpendicular to our street, was the fourth house. It had been the first one built and was by far the largest of the four. In it resided my great-aunt Conchita, her husband, Luis Aragón, and my great-grandmother, Mamamía. In the center of the compound (a suburban *batey*, I just now realize) was a large, common backyard with many different types of fruit trees: oranges, lemons and limes, mangos, mameys, papayas, guavas, bananas, and avocado.

I have sometimes described this setup to North American friends and they have been surprised at how cramped our existence was, what with seven people in one house (eight when the maid's son was born) and all those relatives breathing down one's neck. I never felt lacking for space, nor did my parents, and I can't recall the question ever coming up. If I needed more room, there was the backyard or any of the other houses. They were always open and no one was ever turned away or told to come back at a more propitious time. Privacy, however, was out of the question and therefore never considered; the word wasn't even part of my vocabulary. On the other hand, loneliness did not exist. It was only after arriving in the United States that it became a real emotion and privacy became a necessity. I think the two must be related.

There were added benefits to growing up in an extended family such as mine. For one thing, there were several role models to pick from, on both the male and the female side. I have never since been a part of a group of such radically different individuals. And it wasn't that the members adapted to the group or modified their behavior to fit in, but rather that the group, unstructured as it was, adapted to them and took them in. Furthermore, everyone, successful or not, was on equal footing in the family. Thus, I was able to pick and choose, as my own, those qualities I most admired, not just in my parents but in all my relatives as well.

The compound acted as a center for those who lived in other parts of the city. Aunts and uncles, cousins, and friends came during the week to visit, to talk, to eat, to have coffee, to play cards. On Saturdays and Sundays, it was more common than not to have twenty or thirty visitors dropping by. Except that they weren't visitors. They were family coming home to occupy those niches they had left but were still reserved for them no matter how long they had been away.

Whenever I wanted to be alone, which was not that often, I went to the rear of the yard where, behind the small grove of banana trees, Mamamía had had a chicken coop built. There were no chickens anymore, but the small concrete block structure still smelled faintly of wet down and droppings. No adult went back there, and so I was safe to perform experiments on the lizards and mice I caught without horrifying my aunt Dinorah, who was always spying on me whenever I played close to the house.

There my friend Sergio showed me how to give an injection. Our patient, or victim I should say, was a green chameleon. No sooner had we applied a syringe full of water (stolen from a medicine cabinet) than the thing went into convulsions and died. We then performed an autopsy to "discover" what the poor reptile had died of, and having found nothing out of the ordinary, we put it in a jar full of alcohol and placed that in a prominent place on my sister Silvia's dresser. We expected Silvia to become upset, that was our purpose, but we did not expect her to tell Dinorah, who, as usual, became horrified and made Sergio and me say a rosary that God might forgive us our terrible sin against one of His creatures. Aunt Dinorah never punished us; instead she made us kneel on the tile floor and led us in prayers. It was behavior modification at its worst. After a prayer session with her, we would always vow never to offend her piety again, a vow we tended to forget within a week's time.

Along with her Franciscan concern for the creatures of God, Dinorah had a streak of superstition as wide as a river. On her dresser were at least two dozen statues of different saints and a collection of glass elephants — purported to bring happiness, contentment, and a husband — which my sister and I played with when she was at work. She was also fond of Chinese numerology and played La Charada, the Cuban version of the "numbers," almost daily.

One day she brought home a big, shiny apple and placed it on a makeshift altar over the armoire. Then she called me over. "María Teresito," she said referring to me in her favorite way, which I detested beyond words. "María Teresito, this is a sacred apple. It belongs to the angels. You must not touch it."

The apple remained undisturbed through the night. Apples, though, were expensive items in Cuba and not easily obtained (deliciousness enhanced by scarcity). When my sister and I arrived home from school that afternoon, we spied the apple shining invitingly above us as if it had been sent from heaven. It was too much. Silvia grabbed it, took a bite, and handed it to me. I did likewise and handed it back. And so, bite by bite we ate until only the core was left. We then devised a story that we had heard what appeared to be angels in the room munching on the fruit. We thought first of going in and stopping them, but we decided against it. It was, after all, their apple.

That night before dinner, we heard Dinorah screaming in the bedroom. "Sacrilege! Sacrilege! Where are those children?"

She rushed out of the room and said to us, "Oh, what a great sin! You must pray, you must pray!"

We kneeled in the bedroom. Dinorah sat on one of the beds and led the prayers. We prayed until we did not hear her any more. Looking up, we saw that she had fallen asleep against the wall. We figured God had forgiven us about a half hour before, so we stopped. The next day, with sore knees, we went to the store and bought the nicest looking apple we could find. She was very happy when we gave it to her.

The Quibú River, by which we lived, was little more than a glorified open sewer. It appeared that all the bathrooms of Marianao emptied onto this small maligned river. The water was black, the mud on the banks was slate colored, and most days it stank horribly. Yet the Quibú lured us. All we had to do was cross an empty lot next to Mamamía's house to reach it. There we caught frogs and the few minnows that survived its pestilence. And there, far from adults, my friends and I went to share our knowledge of sexual matters and to fight our wars, coming home mud covered and ready for the shower. On rainy days when it swelled, the Quibú brought strange and marvelous detrita from upriver: gnarled wood, pieces of furniture, decapitated dolls, a dirty book (the best parts of which had faded away), and a dead dog, stiff and bloated, that we unsuccessfully tried to revive by setting it on its legs, but it was missing one of its paws and the carcass kept toppling over.

The Quibú was also my link to the sea. Its mouth was close enough that I could reach it on foot. On calm days the black river water spewed forth from the mouth to be gradually swallowed up by the turquoise of the Caribbean. Sharks came there to feed, their fins churning into the murk, then rushing back out to safe blue as soon as they had grabbed a morsel.

My great-uncle Luis Aragón made a habit of going on evening walks and, when I felt particularly energetic (in spite of his years, he was a brisk walker), I followed along. One clear night, we wound up close to the mouth of the river where we saw a group of five or six people with lanterns hugging the shore in a semi-circle. When we joined them, we discovered what it was they were surrounding. A huge, round fish, wide as I was tall, lay on its side on the seaweed and sand. The moon shone on its black, velvety skin, which rippled as it panted. The group was silent, awestruck and helpless before the dying creature. What to do but wait for its death? After what seemed like a long time, my uncle broke the silence and asked what it was. "A moonfish," someone replied. It was then that I crouched and poked its side with my index finger. The skin bounced and settled. It felt delicate enough to puncture, like night itself. I stood up, startled, afraid, wanting to wash my finger off but the only water was the sea, stained by the river, night, death.

I don't remember anything else about that night, when or how we made it home, or if I told anyone about touching the fish. I don't think I did. When someone I know dies, however, the moonfish returns to mind, panting, staring with its unblinking eye, and its soft, flabby side, easily pierced, like the moon that gave it light.

This area where we lived was still in the process of being developed and, thus, we were surrounded by empty, weed-choked lots, which bred a great variety of creatures we considered pests. There were the ubiquitous chameleons, mice, cockroaches that grew to be two inches long, and armies of frogs that made walking in the dark an unpleasant experience as they had the habit of jumping blindly against one's legs (as a child I always wore shorts).

Crabs came out at night; dirt colored and fierce looking, they had free entrance to the house, open as it was to let the drafts flow freely through. We learned to live with them, keeping our eyes where we stepped. Occasionally we found one under a bed, but they were notoriously shy and kept to dark corners. During wet weather, it was not unusual to find a dozen of them roaming around inside; then it was necessary to sweep them out.

We had spiders, too, which we called Hairy Spiders. When bored, I would catch them and put a pair in a shoe box to see if they would fight or mate, but they did neither, preferring instead to escape. These spiders were black and quite large, about three inches in diameter, and I was at once fascinated and repelled by them. Adults warned me that they gave vicious bites and it was best to stay away from them. It was in my college library, while leafing through a book on arachnids when I should have been studying for a chemistry exam, that I learned that these spiders were a variety of tarantula. Had I known this then, the name tarantula having such deadly connotations, I would have trembled at the mere sight of one. In my ignorance, I found them pathetic, helpless creatures to be caught and released at will.

By far the worst of these quasi-biblical plagues was the mosquitoes. What winter was to Russia, mosquitoes were to Cuba. It is said that what defeated the Spanish armies during the War of Independence was not the spirit of the Cuban *mambises* or the firepower of the American war machine, but rather the dreaded Anopheles, carrier of yellow fever. The American forces themselves suffered many more casualties from the fever than from bullets.

By the time I came onto the scene, however, Anopheles had been eradicated, and only its harmless but extremely bothersome cousins remained. Hundreds of them settled on the white ceiling of the back porch waiting for us to turn on the T.V. and sit. Then they would swoop down to feed, and a chorus of slaps blended with the songs of frogs around us. Sometimes my sister and I amused ourselves by having a contest to see who had killed the most. We lined them up on the dining room table and counted. The winner got to put a match to them.

Eventually, the municipality started a spraying program, which helped somewhat. Every afternoon at dusk, jeeps equipped with large tanks let out clouds of insecticide up and down our street. The mist came right into our living room through the front door and windows, which were almost always open, and the scent lingered for about an hour. I don't know that it was very healthy for us, but I was happy to see the jeeps; they made the evening bearable. When my father was able to afford them, we got air-conditioners for the bedrooms — mammoth machines that sounded like DC-3's at full throttle. At last we could sleep without mosquito netting, that filter which makes everything appear a dull gray in the morning, for the insects disliked the cooled air and we could awaken to a bright, if rattling, room.

The only animals that posed any sort of real threat to us were stray dogs. Mostly they were miserable creatures, more dead than alive, but they struck great fear among us as rabies was still common on the island.

Once, when I went to get my bicycle from the garage, I heard a whimper coming from a corner. I looked and saw a dog, thin and mangy, as sorry a creature as I had ever seen. I raced into the kitchen and told Sagrada the maid about the dog. The two of us went back into the garage and tried to shoo the animal out, but when Sagrada swatted at it with a broom, it growled and snapped at her. Naturally, we panicked. She rushed into the living room, I close on her heels, yelling: "Rabid dog. Rabid dog." There was a great commotion and soon all the women of the family (the men were still at work) were in the house pondering alternatives. My great-aunt Conchita had the presence of mind to lock all the garage doors. The problem was what to do with the rabid hound. Someone suggested calling a dogcatcher, but this was no easy feat. No one knew where to call, and, in fact, several of the women doubted one existed. Nevertheless, a man eventually showed up wearing a semblance of a uniform: cap with a visor on which was stitched some sort of official-looking emblem. He also wore a checkered shirt several sizes too small for his bulging stomach. In spite of his ramshackle appearance, he had a very nice disposition, treating the women respectfully and with deference, so he was given coffee and the situation was explained.

Several of the women were talking excitedly to him trying to describe where the dog was and his condition, although none of them, except Sagrada, had seen him. The man sat calmly through it all, smiling and nodding. When he was finished with the coffee, he stood up and allowed himself to be led to the garage. As soon as he saw the dog, he concluded that it was not rabid, but exhausted and dying. And with the same calm he exhibited in the living room, he slipped a rope around the animal's neck, pulled him out on the street, and tied him to the back of his truck. As he was getting in, I saw my mother hand him something, most probably a tip. Finally, the truck drove off, dog dragging behind it. No doubt by the time it turned the corner the animal was no longer alive. Upon hearing the story that night after dinner, my father commented between yawns that the man had probably dropped the carcass into the river by the bridge.

Spread throughout the city and its outskirts were beach and yacht clubs, which acted as centers of social life for the middle and upper classes. Membership in these clubs depended primarily upon social class, and you could tell a family's status by the club they belonged to. The Biltmore Yacht Club, for example, catered to the nouveau riche, the main qualification for membership being money. The Miramar and the Vedado Tennis served the upper middle class, while the Casino Español, the Club Militar, and the Profesionales, to which we belonged, were bastions of the not-quite-there middle class.

Up Quinta Avenida, not far from where we lived, was the most exclusive club in the city, the Havana Yacht Club. You had to be very rich, very distinguished, and very white to join, so much so that Batista, the dictator himself, had been denied membership because he was a mulatto. The Yacht Club was so powerful that Batista could do nothing to change the Board of Directors' decision. Eventually, he built his own club, a monstrous thing that looked more like a garish hospital than a place of leisure.

East of the Havana Yacht Club was a public resort and beach known simply as La Playa. Here came those who could not afford to join a club — maids, policemen, factory workers, and others of the working class. On the beach side was an amusement park named, of all things, Coney Island, or Coniailan, as we pronounced it. It was a fascinating place and I loved going there because, among other attractions, it had the only roller coaster I knew of in the city, or on the whole island for that matter. The Spanish name for roller coaster, *montaña rusa* or Russian mountain, bears no kinship to the English. It is, however, historically accurate since the ride originated in Russia. At the time I imagined every Russian city to have one of these contraptions and fantasized Russia to be a country full of amusement parks and, therefore, great fun to live in.

The *montaña rusa* itself was in dire need of repair. On close inspection one could see the wooden beams of the structure warping and peeling, a condition that made the experience all the more thrilling: at any moment the thing might come crashing down from under you. By giving the attendant an extra nickel, you could stay on the cart for additional rides. One Saturday, on a dare from a friend, I stayed on ten times. My stomach disappeared and the world was a mad blur of light and color the rest of the afternoon.

The other amusement that vied with the *montaña rusa* as my favorite was El Laberinto de los Espejos or the Labyrinth of Mirrors, a true maze with innumerable halls and cul-de-sacs lined with glass. No matter how lost I got in it, the mirrors always gave me back myself. Some of my friends learned the way out, but I never did. I let them go through first, no matter that I was the rotten egg; then I had the place to myself—and my images! The Labyrinth of Mirrors was my first metaphysical experience with the self.

On the other side of the street from Coniailan was a row of bars and cafés. On the sidewalks, especially at night, streetwalkers often gathered. I watched them and their tricks, eager, nervous young men, get together and walk into one of the bars or else drive off into the depths of the Havanan night. I was too young yet for those adventures, but something deep in me reacted to such scenes and filled my mind and body with the pleasures of unsatisfied longing. My imagination was further enlivened in these matters by my cousin Rigoberto who frequented the bars of La Playa. Older and more experienced than I, he would often take me aside and describe his pickups and the sexual gymnastics he performed with the girls (some of the things he claimed he did and were done to him would require not only the body of an expert contortionist, but the nimblest of imaginations as well). He always ended our talks by promising to take me along on one of his evening outings as soon as I turned fourteen, that magic age when all of us were supposed to jump, as if by miracle, the chasm between boyhood and manhood. When I reached that period of my life, I was attending Jesuit school in New York and praying every day to the Virgin Mary.

English

GIVEN THE PROXIMITY of the United States and Cuba's virtual economic dependence on it, it was natural for English to become the second, and ever more important, language of Havana. Through consumer goods, movies, and sports it had made its way into the everyday speech of the city. Thus we had our cars: Cadilá, Biu, Ohmobíl, Pontiá, Packa, Estudebeique, Plimo; our movie stars: Jongüéin, Rohodson, Betideivi; and in baseball, the national sport, we had *estrái guan, tubéi, tribéi, honrón,* and the always exciting *doble plei.* But nowhere was American cultural and linguistic influence more evident than in nicknames. Instead of the traditional Spanish Paco, Fico, and Ñico, more and more often one heard Frank for Francisco, Freddie for Federico, and Tony for Antonio. In addition, knowledge of English, more so than French or German, was a true mark of culture and status. And in a mercantile city, which Havana had been since its founding, the ability to transact business in English assured one a solid and well-respected place in the business community.

Ever conscious of preparing us for the rough-and-tumble ambience of Cuban society, my parents enrolled my sister and me in an American school located in Vedado, an old and warmly elegant district that could not have been more Spanish with its almond trees and its colonial houses surrounded by wrought iron.

Cathedral School did, I must say, a marvelous job. By the time I was in third grade, I was all but fluent in English and was reading Mark Twain, Dos Passos, and Harriet Beecher Stowe in the original. The curriculum was curiously mixed but well balanced. Spanish grammar and orthography were followed by math taught in English. After recess we took English grammar and Cuban history. In the afternoon we learned American history and had art lessons taught by a Hungarian exile who spoke a most unusual mixture of English and Spanish, resonant with the deep tones of a man who, you could tell from his deeply lined face, knew too much of the world. The day ended with gym and civics (both in Spanish), subjects no one, not even the teachers, took very seriously.

The student body was equally well balanced and it was from my peers that I learned real English, that is, the language of the everyday, the language that is not taught in classrooms. Although Cubans and Americans tended to play and socialize separately, there were times when we couldn't help but be together and, when we mixed, the languages mixed as well. In the Babel of the playground, I was exposed to expressions and vocabulary and, more important, attitudes and points of view, that were to aid me immensely in my amblings through American society.

It was at Cathedral, during an evening gathering of parents, teachers, and students, that I first played a game called "Spin the Bottle." While the adults discussed matters that did not much concern us children, I had somehow found myself in a group of *americanos.* One of the boys, eyes sparkling devilishly, suggested playing the game and, before I had a chance to ask what it was, six of us were gathered together in a circle with a coke bottle spinning in the middle. When the bottle stopped, it was pointing at me. My "punishment" was to kiss any girl in the group. I thought of Dianne Márquez whose sister was my sister's best friend — the semifamilial relation thus freeing me somewhat from the embarrassment of the moment — but I passed Dianne up in favor of a new girl who had just come from the States. She had the whitest skin I had ever seen and eyes the color of the ocean where it deepened and lips as red and thick as strawberries. I crawled toward her on all fours trying to hide the bulge in my pants; I had never kissed a girl before. I was already falling in love.

Shy as I was, and untutored in the rules of the game, my initial reaction was to kiss her on the cheek. That would have been enough to satisfy my innocent desires, but when our faces were inches away from each other, she closed her eyes and puckered her fruity lips. I kissed, merely brushing my lips against hers at first; then I kissed again, this time pressing as hard as I could, just as actors do in the movies. When her head jerked back, I sensed I had violated the protocol of the game. For a moment she looked at me wide-eyed and righteous, then pulled away, leaving me panting and forlorn. I stood up, not caring if any of them saw the lump in my pants — by this point it was a limp lump anyway — and walked away: "Spin the Bottle" was a silly game.

After fifth grade, our parents enrolled us in Ruston Academy in Biltmore, a wealthy district not far from where we lived. I remember my difficult first year there when nothing seemed to make sense, not the teachers, the courses, or the students themselves. All I did was read Salgari, Verne, and any astronomy book I could get my hands on, barely opening school books that did not deal with history or science.

Affordable by middle-class standards, or so it seemed if our parents were able to send us there, Ruston nevertheless had its share of very wealthy students, and it was my interest in astronomy that first brought me in contact with the opulence of the rich. When it was time to do science projects (my knowledge of the subject had become legend in the sixth grade), I paired up with another student who determined he wanted to do a study of the solar system. His name was Eduardo Mestre and he was the son of Goar Mestre, owner of CMQ, the largest and most important chain of radio and television stations on the island. We needed more time than was allotted to us in school to finish our project, so I asked Eduardo to come to my house in order to spend the afternoon working on it.

I had no sooner spied the long black limousine with tinted windows that pulled up in front of our house than I began to feel uncomfortable. The discomfort was heightened by the milk and pastries my mother had decorously set for us on the dining table. She had never put out her good china and lace napkins for any of my other friends. When we had finished our snack, Eduardo asked to see the fine library where I kept all my astronomy books (I had told him in school that I owned tons of them), so I led him to my parents' bedroom where, over the bed, my father kept all the books in the house. I pulled out the ten books on the subject and proudly showed off my collection.

Eduardo was not much impressed, but I was not to understand why until I visited his house in Biltmore a week later. I was met at the door by a maid dressed in black, who escorted me through a labyrinthine house to a double set of heavy, wooden doors, which opened onto a room the size of our living room and dining room combined. Books of all sizes and ages lined the walls. In the center was an oval table at which Eduardo was sitting with a blonde, very attractive lady — his French tutor, I later discovered. Before them on the table was a pile of about fifty books — Eduardo's collection.

From then on we met at Eduardo's house, and although he once suggested, I think out of a sense of fairness, coming to my house, I put that possibility to rest quickly. I much preferred that library, the likes of which I had only seen in Hollywood movies, and the huge house with an almost infinite number of rooms. There was also the swimming pool and, of course, the French tutor of the golden skin and lips like Brigitte Bardot's.

Not everyone at Ruston was as wealthy as Eduardo; in fact, there were a few sons and daughters of the custodial staff who added a certain touch of earthiness to what otherwise would have been an ivory tower (perhaps I should say sand castle as the winds and waves of revolution would, in little more than a year, wash the world of privilege away). Nevertheless, many of my classmates were members of the moneyed classes, children of newspaper editors, businessmen, politicians, and doctors.

There were also many Americans, but at Ruston, unlike Cathedral School, our primary contact with them came during gym, health, shop, and other peripheral classes. By the time I left the school to come to the United States, there were few of them left, as the United States had gradually become the enemy, and all vestiges of American capitalism (which the school, by its very nature, supported) had been eradicated. Even the name of the school was changed, but I do not recall to what.

What I do know is that I learned my second language better than anyone expected and was exposed, if indirectly, to a great deal of American culture, from the game of football to the obsession with holiday decorations to Americans' inborn optimism and generosity, evident to me in the fairness of the American teachers and their concern for their students, no matter what social class they belonged to.

Not so the Cuban teachers. Notwithstanding arguments to the contrary, an educational system, and the people in it, merely reflects the beliefs and values, as well as the prejudices and weaknesses, of the social group it serves. That is why schools in the American south were segregated until recent times. And that is why education in Cuba, particularly in private schools, favored the wealthy: it maintained their values; it urged adherence to their mores; and, most unfortunately, it looked askance at those who had managed to breach the walls of their institutions. Nothing new about this. It happens everywhere, even in the United States, though the effect is less seditious here, if only because public education, even in this age when there are sure signs of its decline (as society becomes less expansive and opportunity less abundant), still allows for a possible way up the ladder of success. In Cuba, public education, admirable as it was in many respects, was not a consideration for the middle class, certainly not in Havana. One had to go to private school, religious or secular. And it was there that I, child of a family that had barely made it in (we had no distinguished surname we could cling to, no money to speak of, and the men, except for a few notable exceptions, were not particularly ambitious in an economic sense, at least not while in Cuba), felt most disarmed.

My one salvation was my grandfather Pablo's notoriety as an intellectual and critic. Once they knew whose grandson I was, Cuban teachers' view of me changed conclusively. I enjoyed the attention and used it to my advantage on more than one occasion. I had my grandfather's name. Why not share the status associated with it? Some of my American teachers no doubt knew of him: he was a brilliant and well-known man. But they were not impressed with me, as I was far from brilliant in the classroom, a fact that became quite clear to me when I found myself attending summer school for having failed English.

While my teachers inspired my admiration for the country to the north in a subliminal way, movies (subtitled) and television (dubbed) added to it much more directly. My heroes, my women, my Helens, my Troy was the United States. What did we Cubans have that could possibly rival the glitter of Marilyn Monroe's lips, the innocence of Debbie Reynolds, the purposeful swagger of John Wayne? Or all those battleships and planes crowding the screens? Or the grit of World War II soldiers with their steely teeth and unshaven faces? Or New York where life was vertical and framed in neon? Or snow or Disneyland or nudist camps or cowboys and Indians or Niagara Falls or Porky Pig? And over it all hung the umbrella of freedom wider than the Cuban sky.

More than anything I wanted to be American and live in a suburb (where I now write from) and have a pretty blonde wife who waited on me as Doris Day waited on Rock Hudson. And I wanted to have children like those spoiled brats of American television and I wanted to own a Buick and have martinis at lunch in a wood-paneled bar surrounded by women dressed in black, and I wanted to be Eliot Ness, self-righteously ridding the world of gangsters and booze; most of all, I yearned for the reality of celluloid, truth of fiction. If not, I wished my life to be as smooth and mellow clear as the clichés I saw parading before me in the Trianón, the Rodi, the Miramar. I was sold.

On the other hand (yin and yang), there was José Martí, whose poetry I memorized and whose life I accepted as a model; there was the music Sagrada the maid played on the radio; and there were carnivals and Nochebuenas and trips to La Luisa and Sunday outings through El Malecón and my bus rides through the city and La Playa with its amusements and its painted women. There was the family, too: raucous, anarchic, unpredictable, joyful, accepting, loving, secure. Pampered and protected as I was within that extended elastic womb, I firmly believed that love was the primum mobile of human existence. I thought everyone was loved by someone else. Exile taught me otherwise. The world was barren and cold outside, and although I learned to survive love-lessness quickly enough (one must in New York) and to appreci-ate my newfound privacy and independence, I often pined (still do) for that little world by the Quibú River, where everything and everyone fit without ever a need for parentheses.

Miguel

MIGUEL MEDINA CAME to Cuba in 1893 or 1894 as a lieutenant in the Spanish army. Whether he was drafted or joined out of his own volition, no one seems to know. But this is unimportant. The fact is that Spain was not a very pleasant country for a young man without money or connections. Its economy was in shambles, its society stagnant and brittle; of its once vast empire in America, only two colonies remained, Puerto Rico and Cuba. Miguel must have been glad to escape the sinking ship.

Yet the situation in which he found himself upon arrival in Havana was no better. The War of Independence was only a year away. To the Cubans, he was an enemy occupying their land; to his superiors, another lieutenant to order about; to his charges, he was a reflection of their own misfortunes and failure to wile or buy themselves out of conscription into an army that was an army in name only. Low morale, inadequate training and equipment, and yellow fever made the Spanish soldiers a poor match against the *mambises* — the Cuban freedom fighters — whose tactics resembled those of modern-day guerrillas.

Keeping a low profile and avoiding combat must have required most of Miguel's resourcefulness. He must have been successful at it since, as far as I know, he never saw the front lines. He even managed to court and marry a Creole, a strong, determined one at that, whose will was made of steel and whose personality was solid rock compared to the wind-blown dust of Miguel's.

In 1898, when the Cubans, with some help from the United

States, defeated the Spanish, Miguel, along with his wife, Cacha, and their three children, were repatriated. Spain, however, was hardly the place to start over. The economy was worse than when he left, its coffers drained by war and mismanagement. Whatever jobs remained were not about to be given to a man who so clearly symbolized the nation's demise.

To worsen matters, Cacha herself was miserable. She had not wanted to leave Cuba and had made her sentiments known vociferously to her husband. In addition, she could not bear the sight of the sister-in-law they were staying with and made no attempt to disguise her feelings.

Miguel, it seems, would have been content to wait the situation out in his hometown of Valladolid, living off his relatives and doing small jobs here and there. Not so Cacha. She had had enough. She herself would go to the Naval Office and plead their case to be given passage back to America. When that did not work, she managed to get an audience with the Queen of Spain. Cacha made sure to bring Pablo, a five-year-old boy then, who had a protuberant, but benign, growth on his neck. The Queen took pity and not only ordered that the Medinas' wish be granted, but also had the royal surgeon operate on my grandfather's neck.

In a few months, the family was in San Juan, Puerto Rico, where Miguel's brother had offered him a job in a sugar mill he managed. The indomitable Cacha had trouble with Miguel's brother, however, and, within the year, they returned to Havana. No sooner had they arrived than Miguel realized his mistake. The war was still fresh in the memory of the island and employers were as likely to hire an ex-lieutenant in the Spanish army as they were to raise the Spanish flag every morning over their offices. Just then, luck showed her face. A friend of Miguel's wrote him urging him to come to Campeche, in the Mexican peninsula of Yucatán. He was the bookkeeper of a rope-making concern and they were looking for a good man.

At last prosperity seemed to shine on them. Miguel's was a natural intelligence and his capacity for work was matched only by his easy-going nature. Before long, he had risen in the ranks of the company to become manager. Cacha, too, settled down. In between children (besides the original three, she bore twelve more in Mexico, five of whom died in infancy), she started selling homemade tacos at a neighborhood bar. Her blend of Mexican ingredients and Cuban seasonings was a novelty in the town, and soon she had a thriving business. When she noticed that much of the drinking water in the neighborhood was polluted by sewage seeping into the wells, she started selling bottled rainwater that she collected in a cistern she had placed on the roof of the house.

But not all was well between the Medinas. Along with his education, his impeccable manners, and his success, Miguel nurtured certain habits that were not to Cacha's predilection. He gambled, he liked to have a few drinks at night, and sin of all sins, he was an inveterate womanizer, coming home late at night penniless, smelling of strong liquor, and smeared with lipstick. My greatuncle Pastor, the last of the male children to die, once told me of being awakened in the middle of his sleep by Cacha's thunderous voice, the crash of glass, and the slam of the front door as the patriarch (if I may call him that) fled his wife's wrath, much preferring the soft embrace of the tropical night. The nightly fights spurred him to come home later, spend more money (sometimes his complete weekly salary) at the races, drink more, chase more skirts. All this made Cacha's rage reach sublime heights until the very house shook.

The children took care of themselves. Busy as Cacha was with her enterprises during the day and her quarrels with her husband at night, she had little time for the brood. From their accounts, though, it was not a bad life. Campeche was a small town, yet as a port on the Gulf of Mexico, it was always full of activity, the streets peopled with sailors and merchants and those who catered to them. Besides, they had inherited their mother's resourcefulness and their father's hunger for knowledge, so that, when they weren't busy making money running errands for neighbors, they immersed themselves in reading. And there were always books around to devour. Miguel made sure of that. As soon as the boys were old enough, they found regular jobs to help support the family. Education, at least of the formal sort, was a luxury. Such was the fate of the two oldest, my grandfather Pablo and Luis, who was, as we shall see, to become head of the family.

Years passed and routine began to weigh on Miguel. His windswept spirit demanded a change. He wrote to a friend in Havana inquiring about the situation there and whether the people, now that Cuba was a full-fledged republic, had softened their attitudes. The friend wrote back that all was clear and there was plenty of money to be made, especially by a man of Miguel's background and experience.

Within the month, Miguel, Cacha, and their ten children were back in Cuba. It had not occurred to Miguel to find a job or to rent suitable quarters; consequently, the twelve of them wound up in a one-room apartment in a *solar,* the typical Cuban slum dwelling. They lived in this room without a bathroom or furniture for a year, yet — this never ceases to amaze me — they not only survived but actually thrived under circumstances most people might consider intolerable.

Finally, Miguel found a good-paying job at a bank and they moved into a large house on Indio Street, which they shared with one of Cacha's sisters and her husband and child. They still had no furniture and the children were sleeping on the floor. Conflicts between Cacha and her sister — my great-grandmother seemed to feed on adversity — forced them to move again, this time to a house on Rayo Street from which they were evicted six months later for failure to pay rent. Miguel had once again fallen into the hands of the three sisters — gambling, drinking, whoring. No matter where they moved, no matter how resourceful Cacha's economizing, the debts grew by geometric progression and Miguel's profligacy followed closely behind. The fighting intensified. He spent more and more time away from home.

Perhaps the troubles were too much for him; perhaps routine and boredom reawakened his Odysseus complex. He finally decided to head north to New Orleans where, it was reported to him, there was plenty of money to be made. Thus, Miguel was on the move again, this time without Cacha, planning to send for her and the children once he settled. Settle he did, in a good job in the sugar industry, and wired passage money back to Cacha.

But the fearsome woman had refused to play Penelope from the moment her husband boarded the steamer. With Miguel's money she paid the mountain of bills that had accrued, afterward sending him a letter demanding that he come home immediately or stay in New Orleans and rot.

Miguel did not return, nor did she receive any response from him. It was then that she asked Pablo, as the first born, to head the family and to take over the responsibilities his father had so casually abandoned. At this time, Pablo was in his early twenties and had been working for several years. He had inherited his father's intelligence and independent spirit, as well as his love for literature and the arts. Always his father's son, he refused, maintaining that it was Cacha who had abdicated her duty: she should have gone with her husband and that was that. He would not side with his mother, nor would he take his father's place.

Had Cacha been a lesser woman, she might have crumbled. Even her oldest son, the one who showed so much promise, had turned against her. The battle lines were set. On the father's side were Pablo, Pastor, and the third oldest, Miguel; on the mother's, all the girls and Alberto. The only one missing from the struggle was Luis, the second oldest male, who had been sent to New York for training by the Cuban Telephone Company.

Luis was Cacha's favorite child. Living in the shadow of Pablo, he felt ignored by the father and had become his complete antithesis: he never drank, never whored, had never come close to a gaming table. He saved all he could and, much to his brothers' derision, was a devout Catholic. When his mother wrote informing him of the situation, Luis abandoned his ambitions and returned home immediately. With what seemed a vengeance, he assumed his father's role. No more unpaid bills, no more throwing away money on light-headed pursuits. Cacha was overjoyed and Luis had his moment of triumph. He had deposed the father. From now on, she would be queen and Luis her prime minister, and those who didn't like it could move, an empty threat if ever there was one as Pablo was already preparing his marriage to my grandmother Juana María and the others were in their late teens, too young and dependent to undermine Luis' new-found authority.

After eight months of silence, Miguel returned to Havana with the illusion that he was still in control of the family. He noticed the cold with which his children received him when he entered the house and his wife's conspicuous absence (she had stayed in the bedroom, boiling as usual). When Luis came home from work, he confronted his father: he had no business in the house. He had abandoned his wife and children and had, therefore, forfeited whatever rights had been naturally his. He had to leave immediately.

The old man was shocked speechless. His family had disowned him, and his own son cast him out into the street without so much as a greeting first. Cacha had had her day.

Miguel stayed in Havana only long enough for the divorce to become final. Then he left for New Orleans, never once looking back. There he found a new wife, and, finally — or so the family maintains — gave up his wanderings and settled.

I never met Miguel; he died in New Orleans a year before my birth, but I remember Cacha well. On several occasions my father took me to her house, an old and gloomy place where it seemed the light of day had never shone. I remember her sitting in a straight-backed wheelchair giving orders to her children. A stroke had paralyzed her and twisted her face so that her lips did not meet evenly, making her kisses quiversome and unpleasant on my cheek. She was missing a few teeth as well and her skin was a mass of wrinkles from which any semblance of warmth had disappeared and turned into a fire simmering just below the surface. Yet her eyes gleamed with power, and she was, everyone knew, the mistress of her household while Luis, her trusted minister, was a dim shadow behind her.

Grandfather Pablo

MY FEW MEMORIES of him come from visiting his house in Cotorro, a suburb of Havana. We — children and grandchildren — would go for occasional Sunday dinners and usually arrived early, while he was still in the city doing his television commentary for a show called *"El Mundo en Televisión."* I remember sitting in his living room with his wife, Victoria, watching him flip through *El Mundo,* one of the principal newspapers of the city, and analyze, or should I say scrutinize, some of the news items. His reports appeared to be extemporaneous and were little more than an excuse to have him speak his fancy. Thus, on any one Sunday, one might hear him discuss topics from the British monarchy to the latest advances in heart surgery with masterful ease, as if he were sitting back in his favorite chair at home. His opinions would be punctuated with quotes from and allusions to Shakespeare, Cervantes, Aristotle, the Koran, and any other source that might pop into his head. I watched proudly: not many boys had brilliant, witty grandfathers like Pablo Medina.

The house was a world unto itself, cluttered as it was with books, record albums, paintings, and memorabilia of a full and active life. A portrait of Beethoven, hanging over the sofa, dominated the living room. His stormy gaze fell on every corner, on every chair, giving the sensation that some dark, overwhelming force was about to be unleashed. There were also statues and busts of the great composers, a leather-bound collection of Jules Verne's works, which I eventually inherited, sea shells, Mexican baskets, photographs of celebrities he had interviewed, and a parrot that spoke beautifully literate Spanish laced with expletives that would put a sailor to shame. Out on the front porch was a big multicolored hammock that my sister and I would climb on and swing until we were vertical.

My favorite part of the house was a room over the garage, which I was in only once when Abuelo Pablo invited me to take a siesta with him. It was a musty place with books lining the walls. I remember there was a double bed and an easy chair; there might even have been a desk. He lit some incense and we both lay down, he covering his face with the pillow, a habit that has been acquired by all the men of the family, including myself. In a few minutes he was blissfully snoring. I, however, was wide awake, entranced by this magical room away from everything and everyone, the sweet smell of incense adding an almost liturgical quality to the moment. Listening to grandfather's wheezes and gurgles, I wanted never to leave this *sanctum sanctorum* where he communed with the spirit of Morpheus.

Grandfather Pablo arrived home usually in the early afternoon, by which time dinner was ready and we, famished by the wait, would cajole him into immediately sitting down to eat. He would complain that he wasn't hungry enough yet and, in order to spur his appetite, would bite into an enormous red chile that looked as if it had been grown in the devil's own garden. Then he would grimace and make faces at my sister and me as he waited for his plate. Watching him eat was a treat in itself; he was a man who not only enjoyed food but also let you know it and shared his delight with those at the table — a true epicure. Those few Sunday dinners at Pablo's house always led me to make meals more than just a filling of my stomach. Of the things I can offer to friends and family, it is food, first and foremost, that I think of.

Pablo married my grandmother Juana María in 1920 when he was twenty-four and she twenty-one. It is said in the family that Juana María had a terrible time of it. Charming as Pablo was, he had nonetheless inherited his father's insatiable appetite for women, horses, and the high life. That he sometimes came home without his paycheck, having lost it at the races, other times smelling of women and liquor, as his father had done before him, was no great matter to him. Bills could wait and there was always money to be made the following week. It fell on Juana María to scrounge for money among her family in order to pay rent, the grocer, the children's school. At times she was forced to pawn jewelry and furniture.

Pablo's notorious restlessness added insult to injury. He changed jobs almost as often as he changed suits. When the routine of a particular position became overbearing, he quit, went home, and announced it as coolly as he would a bit of political news he'd heard on the street. And every time this happened, my grandmother told me between puffs of her cigarette, she wanted to die. More than once they went hungry; more than once they were forced to move from good, roomy homes to cramped, roach-filled apartments on the fringes of the slums. Abuelo Pablo worked at one point or another in his life as an office manager for a legal firm, a secretary, an accountant for a sugar mill, fiscal director for Kraft of Cuba, and chief managing officer for Myrurgia, a Spanish perfume firm. All of these positions, and others too numerous to list (my uncle Carlos once calculated that Pablo had held forty different jobs in his life), he left because the initial challenge that had fed his enthusiasm fizzled away.

All except for one, that is. While he was with the perfume firm, Pablo was given the responsibility of expanding the business into the United States. The owners provided him with a hefty sum of money for the enterprise. Pablo was elated. Here was a challenge worthy of his talents! He planned his trip so that on his way to New York, where the firm's fathers determined they should establish their central office, he would stop off in New Orleans and pay a visit to his father, Miguel. While there, a brilliant idea occurred to him. What better way to announce the entry of Myrurgia Perfumes into the North American market than to have the New Orleans symphony perform an all-Spanish music concert under the sponsorship of the company? Pablo, knowledgeable as he was in classical music, organized the program and selected the pieces to be played.

The concert was a huge success. It was well attended and the newspapers had nothing but praise for the organizers and promoters of the event. There was a small cloud amidst all the sun-

light, however: it turned out that Pablo had spent every last cent
of the allocation on the concert. He never made it to New York,
instead returning to Havana with his pockets full of newspaper
clippings and congratulatory telegrams from everyone of note in
the city, including the mayor and the president of the chamber of
commerce. The owners of Myrurgia, who had already received
news of the grand event and were understandably outraged, met
Pablo with his dismissal papers. Pablo signed them and unre-
morsefully walked out.

For the most part, however, my grandfather's employers were
not only pleased but also quite impressed with his performance
and his capacity for work. Most of them were, I've been told,
sorry to see him go.

Twenty years ago, at a party given by a girl I was dimly thinking of courting, I was introduced to a Cuban gentleman, bent and
brittle with age, who, upon hearing my name, asked me if I was
related to the music critic.

"He was my grandfather," I answered.

"Boy," he continued, still holding my outstretched hand and
raising his left over his head, "you should be proud you are his
grandson. He was a brilliant man. I should know: he was my personal secretary for three years."

He then went on to tell me that he had hired my grandfather
with the understanding that he was an experienced stenographer.
Pablo, however, did not know a whit about stenography. He had
lied about his experience so convincingly, mentioning companies
he had worked for and bosses he had had, that the old gentleman
hired him on the spot.

"I thought I would check his references later on, but I never got
around to it."

"How did you discover he didn't know shorthand?" I asked
him.

"One day about six months before he resigned I was rummag-
ing through his desk trying to find something or other — he was
away, it was hard to keep him sitting for very long — when I noticed that his stenography pad was full of doodles, with an occasional word written down here and there. I was shocked! Every
letter he had ever typed for me was perfect — just the way I had

given it to him. Next day as I was dictating, I walked around my desk and stood behind him. He didn't budge, just kept doodling. I said, 'Sr. Medina, that is the strangest shorthand I have ever beheld. You told me you knew stenography.' And then he said, 'If I'd told you I didn't, you wouldn't have hired me.' When I asked him what his trick was, he said he memorized my dictation, then typed it out before he forgot. Imagine! He had a photographic memory.

"Six months later he came in one morning and resigned. I tried to make him stay — offered him a raise, vacation time, a private office, but it was no use. You couldn't keep a man like Pablo at a job like that. He'd had enough. He was the best secretary I ever had. A few years later I heard him on the radio talking about Brahms and Mozart and things I'd never heard of before. I tell you, you should be proud. Men like that come around once in a hundred years."

I wasn't surprised. I had heard many stories, particularly from Carlos, about Abuelo Pablo's intellectual prowess. He had, for example, memorized whole sections of *Don Quixote* and could recite them at will. His mind was a vast repository of human knowledge and endeavor — mathematics, literature, music, food, history, philosophy — instantly available whenever he wanted to make a point. And because Pablo knew so much, he could lie very well, for no one dared challenge him. Not that he lied often. Let us just say that he could bluff his way through any situation and come out ahead in the end. Yes, I think this last statement might just summarize the way he dealt with reality.

Radio was the one constant in his life, at least from 1930 on. That was the year when my great-uncle Luis Aragón arranged for him to be a panelist in "La Bolsa del Saber," a radio show Luis emceed. The show consisted of a four-member panel who attempted to answer questions on any topic mailed in by the listeners. Pablo and Juan Luis Martín, another Renaissance man and a linguist who was conversant in twenty-two languages, including seven dialects of Chinese, were the permanent members, while the other chairs rotated among university professors, politicians, and specialists in specific fields. In the rare instance when no one on the panel was able to answer the question before it, the

listener was sent a gift — a book, or tickets to a concert or the theater. Most of the time, however, the questions were answered. Luis
Aragón made sure of that by padding the panel with the best
minds in Havana.

The show was a huge success and there were several reasons
for this. Cubans had a great deal of admiration for men whose
knowledge bridged the whole spectrum of human behavior. In
this sense we were still very much in the Renaissance, far behind
the society of the North where specialized practical knowledge —
that which brought great advances in medicine, agriculture, space
exploration, and kitchen gadgetry — was, and still is, held as the
ultimate goal for the learned man. The Cuban audience was more
than willing to listen to four highbrows expound on everything
under the sun, no matter that it was not utilitarian, out of sheer
admiration and awe and perhaps with the dim hope that they
might learn something themselves. The men involved in "La
Bolsa del Saber" did not answer with a simple yes or no or a date
or geographical location as if they were computer-minded autom-
atons. More often than not, questions that required simple answers led to lengthy expositions on the subject matter. Thus the
question, "Who was Napoleon's most trusted advisor?" would
lead into Ney's biography with a sprinkling of anecdotes regarding his private life thrown in to perk the listeners' interests and
keep them tuned in. According to the consensus, Pablo was a master at this, something I can easily understand having watched him
years later on television gracefully and confidently discourse on
matters he might have prepared five minutes ahead of time.

In short, these men were entertainers as well as sages. The
most interesting element of the show, which kept it on the air for
over ten years, was the interplay of the different personalities that
participated. Whenever there was disagreement on a given answer, discussions among the participants and the emcee ensued.
At times, these discussions turned into heated arguments.

The debates between Luis and Pablo were particularly vehe-
ment, due, no doubt, to the differences in their personalities.
Luis, on the one hand, was a forthright man of traditional values,
a gentleman in the old sense, kindly but stern, and at times somewhat righteous. Pablo, on the other hand, was a consummate

bohemian whose absolute self-assurance made him rise above tradition and whose humility was an obsolete appendage to his ego. When uncle Luis challenged one of Pablo's answers, sparks flew, for my grandfather was not a man to be outdone easily. "Your answer is incorrect, sir," Luis would say. "Your research is shoddy, sir." Then Luis would quote from the books he consulted (many of which were present in the studio for quick on-the-air reference) while Pablo sat back smiling like the Cheshire cat. This attitude, my grandmother claimed, infuriated Luis all the more. "It would appear that Mr. Medina considers himself more knowledgeable than these gentlemen who have spent a lifetime studying the subject." At this point, Pablo would quote, from memory, his source, and give chapter and page number to boot. This sort of bickering back and forth between them sometimes continued through the remainder of the show. If no solution was reached, the other panel members consulted a specialist and a conclusive answer was given the following week. Sometimes Luis was right, sometimes Pablo. Rarely, said my grandmother, lighting another cigarette, did either one admit defeat at the hands of the other.

At first, the directors of the radio station were quite anxious about these unrehearsed skirmishes on the air (the show was live), but when they discovered that a significant portion of the audience was tuning in expecting the unexpected, they relaxed and let the show go on in its original format, with Aragón and Medina battling each other. Much as Luis and Pablo disliked one another personally, something must have existed between them that kept them working together over many years. Yes, they were related by law, having married sisters, but I doubt that was it. More likely, it was a mutual respect and recognition of each other's intelligence and accomplishments that allowed for this sort of civilized antagonism without personal attacks or the slightest tinge of envy.

When my grandfather first became involved with it, radio was a very young medium. Until 1941, when he went into the field full-time, he was not salaried, doing his shows after work or during his lunch hour. In a few instances, he was able to convince whatever employer he was working for at the time to sponsor a show. Other times, he asked listeners for donations, much like public broadcasting does nowadays. Besides participation in "La Bolsa del Saber," for which he was paid a meager honorarium, he hosted a "commentary" and a classical music hour. The directors at La Cadena Azul, the radio station he was associated with most of his professional career, allowed him to do pretty much as he pleased in these shows, such was the respect they had for his abilities to inform and entertain, and, above all, to draw and keep an audience.

His commentaries, which were later collected in the one book he ever published, *Medinadas*, varied greatly in theme. Whatever piqued his interest that particular week made its way onto the show. Sometimes he analyzed literature or the arts; other times, he talked philosophy or religion; when he felt like it, he included a recipe or two, or notes on the language, or tongue twisters. One particular entry, entitled "Soy Abuelo" ("I am a Grandfather"), relates what it means to be a grandfather and to have a grandson bearing his name. He wrote this piece on 10 August 1948, the day after my birth. Little did he know then that thirty-seven years afterward I would be writing about him.

Besides music, the field he loved to study and talk about, and to which he would dedicate much of his air time in later years, was geography. One essay in his book deals with a trip he took as a teenager on a sailing schooner that circumnavigated the Yucatán peninsula. Another is a description of dawn over Havana. In two others, one about Chichén Itzá during the height of Maya civilization, the second on ancient Athens, he emulated Jules Verne, a writer he much admired for his ability to describe places he had never visited. In both of these, there is the same sense of place one finds in those based on his actual experiences. In all of them a strong narrative style is evidenced. He wrote with confidence and simplicity and with no literary aspirations whatsoever.

Given its nature, his show on music was significantly more structured. Usually he would play certain compositions and then describe and illustrate their origins, their strengths, their weaknesses, where and when the different instruments came in, and when they left. The show, I've been told by people old enough to have been devoted listeners of his, was a minicourse in musical theory. But far from being a dry and scholarly lecturer, he liked to lace his discussions with gossip and apocryphal anecdotes about the composers' lives. Thus, after playing parts of Schubert's Unfinished Symphony, he went on to narrate how the young insecure composer visited the old master Beethoven with the incomplete work. After studying the wrinkled and stained music sheets, Beethoven gave his opinion: "It is not worth finishing."

When Pablo disliked a composer — and he especially disdained Cuban composers, particularly Lecuona, whom he considered more farsical than classical (a dangerous thing to say as Lecuona was then at the height of his fame) — he did such a masterful job of destroying their music that sales of their recordings actually went down in the capital. In one instance, he brought the ire of the Cuban musical industry on himself by claiming that Lecuona was nothing more than a plagiarist, proving his point on the air by playing a piece, identical to the one Lecuona claimed as his own, apparently written by a Mexican composer of the nineteenth century.

Pablo's devotion to radio was little else than an extension of his devotion to himself. Broadcasting in the Cuba of the 1930s was a haphazard affair. As I've said, the medium was still quite young and thus allowed a great deal of freedom and experimentation with few regulations hampering creativity. For a man of great creative energy and a superhuman ego, nothing could be better. In other occupations he was forced into in order to survive, Pablo mattered only in relation to the welfare of the company or the sugar mill or his immediate boss. In the end, any excuse would serve to quit this type of job. Radio, on the other hand, afforded him the opportunity to be himself and to have others like him for doing so.

If his personality shone through the air waves, it was another matter at home. My father tells me that he was, for the most part, a kindly man, yet aloof and moody. He came and went when he pleased, concerned himself with their welfare only when it occurred to him, and no amount of pleading from my grandmother or, when she realized pleading didn't work, yelling made him change his ways. When at last Juana María found him walking down the street hand in hand with another woman, she flew at him with all the pent-up rage and frustration of sixteen years.

Pablo left, went to Mexico, and was not heard from for three months. That was the end of the marriage. And he turned from the experience with much the same cavalier attitude he quit his jobs.

Yet he was forgiven. I have never heard my aunt Chala or my uncle Carlos speak ill of him. My father, who being the oldest was most affected by the divorce — he had to go to work at fifteen to help support the family as Pablo never sent a penny of support money — refers to him with no small amount of admiration. My great-aunt Conchita, who, along with her husband, Luis, also had to take the responsibility of helping Juana María out, has told me more than once what a great man Pablo Medina was. Even late in her life, my grandmother admitted to anyone who dared to ask that she still loved him. Only in a handwritten biography she gave to me as a child, and which I now have in my possession, did she give vent — very subtly, almost as if she meant for me to gloss over it — to any negative emotions regarding her ex-husband. At the end of a paragraph devoted to him, she writes: "Your grandfather was endowed with a prodigious memory and infectious wit. He was also charming and vibrant. Wherever he went, people noticed him and deferred to him. He never cared about his children or about you. He only cared about himself."

My grandfather Pablo died on my father's birthday. My sister and I were not told of it and we found the news out indirectly. I remember that there was a phone call early in the morning. I knew it was bad news because my father, who was in bed recovering from a gall bladder operation, left almost immediately. We were sent to school as if nothing had happened but, for me at least, the day was a total waste of time. The heavy pall of anxiety blurred the pages of my books and my concentration was tied up in knots. We did not know the news of his death until the following day at Juana María's when we saw the report of the wake and funeral on television. The last image I recall was my father standing by the grave, his head bowed low in sorrow. I walked outside and went to the grove by the chicken coop. There, away from everyone, I cried for him whom I had known so little, and I cried for myself, feeling for the first time the gray milk of mortality spreading over everything until there was nothing but solitude and a dark, moonless night.

The Medinas: standing at left is Luis; the Harold Lloyd look-alike at center is Pastor; Cacha, in control, is seated at far right; Pablo is missing (1927).

Pablo remains a mystery and, as such, somewhat dimmed by time and geography. I have, like the rest of the family, chosen to like him and have given his legend the benefit of my doubts. To damn him, to question or judge his life when others closer to him have not fallen into that trap, would be to condemn the only thing he passed on to me — his name.

El Caballero

I WAS DIGGING by Mamamía's rosebushes. Someone had told me, or I imagined, that the remains of an old Spanish galleon were buried there. Now, during the hour of the siesta when the adults were safely nestled in the hands of Morpheus, I could work undisturbed, dirtying myself, oblivious to the heat and the bees. Not finding anything, I dug deeper hoping to uncover a piece of eight, a burnished sword, a broken musket, some article that might justify my efforts. Bent over into the hole as I was, I felt a tap on my lower back, and it wasn't like any tap I knew (I could recognize the hands of those close to me: my parents, relatives, the maids — I had been touched often enough). This was a stranger's tap, light and formal, almost humble — begging forgiveness for the interruption.

I thought of ignoring it as one might ignore a call, make believe one hasn't heard, in hopes that whoever it was, Grand Interruptor, might disappear. Playing ostrich, however, seemed a ludicrous tactic. Could I convince the tapper I hadn't felt? Not without difficulty — the hole was narrow and I was in almost to the waist — I raised my head and rolled my body sideways onto my elbow, shielding my eyes against the sun with my free arm so I could better see.

Leaning over me and offering a postcard of the Blessed Mother was the one figure that, had I been consulted, I would not have wanted present: El Caballero de París.

He was, as I had always seen him from a safe distance, wearing a long, white robe. He had matted shoulder-length, white hair yellowed at the edges and a beard that radiated outward over his chest. Somewhere between his cheeks, a set of darkened teeth smiled at me.

In the scorching afternoon heat I felt the ice of fear in my veins. The man kept shoving the postcard closer to my face, bobbing his head up and down, as if saying, *Take it.* His fingernails were black with soot and his fingers as thin and veiny as a prophet's.

El Caballero was a phantom of Havana; he walked the streets of the city quoting from the Bible and offering people flowers and postcards. Unpredictable as the sea breeze, he would be in Regla one day, in Jaimanitas, miles away in the other direction, the next. Most people thought him crazy and many parents used him as a threat whenever children misbehaved or refused to eat their dinners: "If you don't eat, El Caballero de París will come and take you away!" After years of hearing about him and having him pointed out as we drove by — much as people will point to a historical monument or a strange bird — I reacted as any healthy child would: I ran as fast as I could to Mamamía, who was sitting in her rocking chair saying her rosary. Sobbing uncontrollably, I buried my face in her lap.

When I look back on him now, it appears his reputation was totally undeserved. He was a truly gentle man who took Christian doctrine literally. No doubt he believed himself to be a true disciple of Christ. His clothes, his flowers, his voice, his extreme humility, were all evidence of a pure quixotic nature, undaunted by the reality around him. He took the teachings of Christ literally: he ate little, had no possessions other than his robe and sandals, and forgave all — insults, disdain, fear. He was too much to take. He was mad, *un loco.* Perhaps it was his absolute goodness that so terrified me.

And, sad irony, his name, given to him because he was so eccentric, so foreign a character in our city, was the best example of a misnomer I have ever encountered. El Caballero de París, Le Monsieur de Paris, was the name given to the guillotiner during the French Revolution.

I don't know if El Caballero is still alive, if he still roams the witch-waters of Havana streets. The last I heard: when police authorities picked him up and were about to intern him in a mental hospital, Castro interceded — unpredictable move from an unpredictable man — and allowed him to go free.

May he walk the streets forever!

Carlos

"*SE ARMÓ EL ACABOSE,*" I heard my father say when we saw uncle Carlos in a rowboat coming toward us.

It had rained heavily and long and now the water in the backyard was a foot deep and threatening to flood us out of the house. Carlos was singing "Río Manzanares" or some such song about high waters and when he noticed us helplessly gathered at the door, he stopped rowing, stood up and waved a bottle of whiskey until he almost tipped the boat over, laughing himself into a coughing fit. We could not help but laugh along, forgetting our predicament. Thus Carlitos, our Noah, saved us. As we headed to Mamamía's house, which was on higher ground, he recited in high declamatory manner a poem I was to memorize years later, "Canción del pirata" by Espronceda, the Spanish romantic.

In a family full of lovable eccentrics, Carlos was, still is, the most endearing. He entered through the door in a whirlwind of hellos and smiles, slightly hunched, his eyes searching for someone to greet, arms flailing outward in every direction. The sun always seemed to shine on him, or, rather, he brought the sun with him. When he appeared, unannounced as usual, a fresh breeze blew through the house, and, no matter my mood, his presence was enough to excite me, as if a switch had been thrown and the world turned funny and interesting and fresh. He had much the same effect on other people, for he even brought a smile to the face of Pepe, one of the most taciturn and serious of my relatives.

Carlos was an incurable practical joker and no one was beyond his tricks. Once he involved my friend Sergio and me in one of his jokes. Someone had given us a pack of firecrackers and we had been setting them off in the yard when it occurred to Carlos that we should place one under my uncle Gustavo's door as he was taking his siesta. The idea immediately appealed to us — after all it had been suggested by an adult — even though we were well aware that Gustavo's naps were sacred and any disturbance during that holy time was bound to spark one of his legendary fits of temper. Carlos even gave us a bean pot to place over the firecracker in order to increase the volume of the racket. When the thing went off, we fled as fast as our feet could carry us, turning only once to see Carlos squirming with laughter on our back porch.

We hid the rest of the afternoon under Mamamía's bed. She checked on us occasionally, bringing us snacks and juice and reporting on the state of Gustavo's search. Initially, he had chased after us in his underwear but, realizing his condition in the middle of the yard, returned to the house to put on some pants. His modesty, she claimed, had saved us from a good beating. The rest of the relatives, well aware of our hiding place and perhaps appreciating the joke themselves, had covered for us. It wasn't until late afternoon that Mamamía told us the coast was clear. Hours under the bed had made us stiff and weary. To this day I don't know who the joke was really on.

And it was Carlos who put a hose through the window of my parents' bedroom in hopes of waking my father and instead drenched my grandparents, who had come from the farm for a visit and had just lain down for a rest. Carlos glowed with embarrassment and he apologized to the lees, but they were not upset. My grandfather especially appreciated the joke, or its intent. No one could be angry at Carlos. He was the black sheep of the family, the *pícaro* with a heart of gold.

Carlos taught me many things. From him I learned my first off-color jokes, how to play poker and how to cheat at it, and, when I was older, how to enjoy drink. Thus I was able to temper the serious pragmatism I inherited from my father with a healthy dose of hedonism. He also taught me something I am just beginning to understand: it is better to take life as a party than as a funeral. Even when your circumstances are such that they lead inexorably to a vision of life as a long, dreary wake, you might as well stop and note that the dead man looks better dead than alive, or that between sobs the eyes of the widow dart about the room a bit much. For there to be dark there must also be light, and vice-versa. Or so the Bible says or implies or ought to.

My uncle was a great storyteller and for hours I would sit and listen to him relate his adventures in the Plaza del Vapor, where he liked to play baseball, and in the dimly lit, smoke-filled bars frequented by sailors and members of the Havana underworld; or else he would tell me a family anecdote. No doubt some of these stories were fabrications and others were greatly exaggerated (the mark of a true storyteller). It did not matter to me then, nor does it matter now that I have heard them several times over. They are part of the family tapestry, tightly woven threads that lead ineluctably to me. One of these stories shows Carlos at his best, or worst, depending on your point of view.

After my parents were married, Carlos became quite friendly with my mother's side of the family. Every so often he would visit my grandparents, Fiquito and Mina, in the country and romp around the town with my mother's cousins, going from party to dance, dance to party, sometimes right through the night. When it was time for him to leave, the cousins would come as a group and plead with him to stay another day or two. More often than not, Carlos acceded, sometimes extending his stay for a week, no matter that he had a job to go to back in Havana.

During one of these visits, Carlos was invited to a dance at the Liceo, the town's social club, where he noticed that one of the girls had yet to dance a single piece. She was as fat as a cow with calf and wore a sad, bovine expression on her face. Pitying her, he went to where she was standing and courteously asked to have the next number. According to Carlos, she was a surprisingly good dancer and so he asked for the next dance and the next. At the end of the evening, he took leave of her, never expecting to see her again.

The following evening after supper, when the family was sitting on the front porch talking themselves drowsy, the fat girl showed up. Convivial as ever and totally oblivious to the girl's designs, Mina asked her to sit by Carlos. And so my uncle spent the whole evening with the girl next to him like an overweight buzzard (his words) eyeing him, nodding agreement at his every word, blinking like a doll whose eyes have lost their springs. She came by the following night and the night after that. By the fourth day the family had the seat next to Carlos reserved and gleefully awaited her arrival to see him squirm and roll his eyes and look at them in desperation. The girl, by the way, happened to be a prude, priggish and insouciant to an extreme. "I'll fix her," Carlos said at supper. Mina warned him to behave; she would not have any funny stuff. Carlos assured her that he would not lay a finger on the girl.

When the appointed time came, Carlos sat on his rocking chair smoking a cigarette, waiting. My aunts Minita and Dinorah and about five or six of the cousins hid behind the door where, if they couldn't see, they could hear what was about to happen. Soon the girl arrived and, sitting next to Carlos, inquired where the rest of the family was.

"I asked them if I could have a few moments alone with you," answered Carlos looking into her eyes.

Then he leaned toward her and when his face was inches away from the now-panting mountain of lard (his words), he let out what was, according to the witnesses behind the door, the loudest fart in the history of Pedro Betancourt.

The girl stood up, the rings of fat under her cheeks now quivering with embarrassment and indignation and yelled, *¡Puerco!* (pig) down at Carlos before turning and walking off the porch, creating a partial eclipse of the setting sun (his description) on her way.

The story spread through the town like cane fire and people told and retold it for years afterward, always concluding the tale with the words: *Ese Carlos es la pata del diablo* (That Carlos is the devil's hoof). When I greet cousins I haven't seen in years, the inevitable reference arises: "How is your uncle Carlos? I remember the time when one of the girls in town took a liking to him . . ."

Carlos once told me that when he dies and comes to judgment, God won't know what to do with him. Paradise is out of the question, and hell, a place he'd like to tour *a la* Dante, he can talk himself out of. He could try to sneak into Limbo, but he claims that his hairy and saggy testicles would give him away. I think a good place for him would be on this side of the Gates of Eden, showering the women with flatteries and, with the most deadpan of expressions, warning the men about St. Peter's pederastic tendencies, after laughing himself into one of his coughing fits.

Mamamía

SHE DIED IN Miami in 1969. Expected as her death was — she had been ailing for two years — Mamamía was deeply mourned by all of us. She was our center, the one person whom we all, without exception, respected and to whom we deferred in family matters. Everyone in our family has sometime borne the resentment of another, has been slighted, envied, satirized. Not Mamamía. She was above any of it. Her presence was holy and it touched whoever was next to her. She died softly, as she had lived, and her spirit flew out to all of us, gave itself up so that we could gain. The last time I saw her, in 1968, she said to me, "I am waiting for it. I am ready." She spoke as if she were awaiting another visitor, then was silent, and her eyes turned in looking for death.

Her real name was Rosalía Romero. Born in 1872, in Pinar del Río, the island's westernmost province, her early years were quiet and peaceful, laced with all the middle-class amenities her merchant father could provide — a good home, the best clothes, sewing classes, and a respectable place in society.

In 1895, that genteel provincial society exploded. Spanish rule had become intolerant. As happens with any colonial power that blinds itself to the inevitability of history, Spain attempted to quelch the rebellious Creoles through extreme and random violence. But Cubans were aflame with the need for liberty and the Spaniards discovered too late the futility of trying to put the fire out with clubs. The armies went back and forth. In the middle were the civilians, and in Pinar del Río, civilians had a particularly bad time of it. When the province's capital city was besieged by the Spanish army and the surrounding countryside ravaged so that food became dangerously scarce, Rosalía's parents decided to leave for Havana, where it was still safe, by any means possible.

After days of looking for someone daring enough to cross the Spanish lines — the penalty for such was death by garroting — the father found a teamster who, for an undisclosed but, doubtless, sizeable amount of money, agreed to drive them to Havana in an oxcart. Traveling only at night and hiding during the day, they and another family (a total of thirteen people) made it to the city in a week's time. It was, Mamamía once told me, a harrowing trip. All they had to eat was condensed milk and a case of canned sardines. The remains of battles were all around them — the bloated corpses of Spanish soldiers whose eyes had been plucked out by vultures, and a few live ones too, writhing in agony from yellow fever. She had wanted to help them, going so far as to get off the cart and giving one of them water, but the teamster put a stop to that. "Anyone who helps a Spaniard is not getting on this cart again." Above all, the fear of being discovered stalked them constantly. The Spaniards, demoralized and exhausted as they were, would kill them instantly. The group made it safely to the capital. On the way back, however, the teamster was found out and executed.

Once the Romero family settled from their ordeal, the war receded into the background and more mundane matters occupied their minds. Foremost among these was the worry that Rosalía, their oldest daughter, now in her twenties, was still without a husband. If she didn't find herself a man soon, very soon, she would remain a maiden forever. Normally this would not have concerned them too much. After all, the odds were against marrying off all four daughters in wartime. But she was their favorite and the one on whom they had expended the most energy. Beautiful, graceful, and as loving a daughter as parents could ever hope for, it would be a shame not to have her grace a man's life.

And it was in the midst of this anxiety, which remained unspoken but was nonetheless felt like a strain of sad cloth in the house and brought a melancholy tone to the parents' voices, that a suitor appeared: a fine young man with blue, determined eyes, thick auburn hair, and a broad, intelligent forehead. His name was Antonio Unanue Chaudiere. He was of Basque and French lineage, well educated, and coming along quite successfully in the business world. They married only a year after the courtship began, and while social protocol suggested a longer period of time, the family was more than glad that Rosalía was at long last spoken for. A year later, the marriage bore its first fruit, my grandmother Juana María.

I learned of Mamamía's life in the afternoons after school. I'd sit on the cool tile floor next to her rocking chair and she would rock herself into the past and narrate her memories. It was history come alive for me. In school I had read of the effects of yellow fever on the Spanish army, but I did not understand until I saw, through Mamamía's words, the armies of the king retreating through her town with their jaundiced faces, their eyes swollen with fever, and their pants wet and stinking from diarrhea. And I had studied about the exploits of Antonio Maceo, the great mulatto general of the War of Independence, but she had actually seen him on his white horse at the head of a column of *mambises*. While the column was stopped in front of her house, she brought him a cup of coffee. She described that, as he bent down to hand her back the empty demitasse, she noticed that a few drops had stained his white *guayabera,* but she dared not say anything. "He had a thick moustache and he smelled of sweat and gunpowder, but his hands were soft, almost delicate, not at all like a soldier's." The textbooks gave me names and dates; her stories gave me pictures.

Besides her experiences during the War of Independence, she also liked to talk about the thirties and her life during Machado's dictatorship. At the time the family (twelve people in all) was living in an apartment on Lealtad Street in the old section of Havana, with the only regular income provided again by my great-aunt Conchita and uncle Luis. Even with their help, Mamamía could barely make ends meet. Juana María had her hands full taking care of the children and trying to keep her marriage from crumbling. Lolita, the youngest, was preparing to wed. The two sons, Ñico and Gustavo, were studying law at the university. In addition, the number of people living under that same roof was continually swelling with fellow students the brothers brought home to hide from the government's secret police.

From 1929 to 1933, when Machado's regime was deposed, there had been a great deal of revolutionary activity in the city. Among the vanguard, involved in terrorist acts against the police, demonstrations, and general strikes, were the students of the university, particularly those enrolled in the School of Law, whose professors were often deeply immersed in the rocky politics of the island. Machado, I must add, ruled with an iron hand, and it is not for nothing that he was known as "the butcher." Many people were imprisoned, tortured, and executed by the police, and toward the end of his rule, all schools and universities were closed.

Fueled by the frenzy of clandestine activities and all the dangers associated with them, and driven by a legitimate ideal — that of reestablishing a constitutional democracy — my two great uncles joined the struggle, planning demonstrations, distributing pamphlets, running money and guns, and whenever necessary offering their home, or rather Mamamía's, as a hideout.

What amazes me, now that I live a sedentary and secure life in suburban America, is that Mamamía not only acquiesced but actually treated whatever friends Ñico and Gustavo brought home as members of the family, no matter that they added a further economic strain on the household, not to speak of the constant anxiety that the police could, at any moment, discover their hideout. Some stayed a week, others a month. One, Cándido Mora, was to hide out with the family for almost three months.

I saw Cándido Mora only once, in Mamamía's house, and that only briefly. He was short, stocky, and balding and he reminded me more of a Galician grocer than an ardent revolutionary. At that time, he was a corrupt senator and his ardor was nothing more than a memory. Looking at him then, when I did not yet know of his escapades as a young man, I would never have imagined that at one time he had singlehandedly confronted six policemen in a shootout and had put them to flight. It was this action that had led to his "stay" with the family.

Unlike most of the other "boarders," however, Cándido felt obliged to offer some sort of payment for the family's kindness. It was thus that he became my father's mathematics tutor. From my father, I learned that he was an excellent, if eccentric, teacher, as eager to teach him algebra as a system for winning in black jack. He was a kindly man in his own way, always giving my father some pennies for candy after the lessons were finished or bringing groceries to the house after one of his evening forays. He was a gentleman, too, treating the ladies of the house, especially Mamamía, with the utmost respect. His blend of kindliness and grace, on the one hand, and fearlessness and bravado, on the other, made him, according to those who knew him, a fascinating character.

On this point my father tells the following story. One Saturday late in the afternoon, Cándido gave him the usual pennies and my father rushed to the store only to find that it was closing and the grocer, an especially unpleasant and grouchy Chinese fellow, refused to serve him. When Cándido found out the problem, he said to my dad, "Come, you'll get your sweets." They knocked several times until the owner responded. No sooner had the Chinaman opened the door than Cándido put a revolver to his temple and said, matter-of-factly, "The boy wants some sweets." Needless to say, my father got his candy.

Everyone in the family agrees that the primary reason my great-uncle Gustavo and Cándido were such close friends was that they were completely and irrevocably crazy. Their involvement in political activities derived as much from their devotion to lofty (and therefore dim) ideals as from a sense of adventure and the need young men often have of looking death in the face. In this they were not much different from most of the revolutionaries that have held sway in Cuban politics. Let the old professors profess the ideals and the young die for them. In the Cuba of the 1930s, when governments came and went, in some cases overnight, and ideologies buffeted the island like storm winds, the anarchy of the young seemed the only political constant and Gustavo and Cándido were in the middle of it.

If Cándido was the eye of the storm, Gustavo was the whirlwind. He was loud and gregarious and he had quirks on top of quirks. When he studied for exams, for example, he crawled on top of the armoire, pulled a heavy blanket over himself (regardless of how hot it was), and stayed there until he felt ready, every once

From left: Juana María, Mamamía, Conchita, Antonio Unanue and, on the hobbyhorse, Ñico (1903).

Then he looked away, shaking his head as if trying to wake from a bad dream, and left.

The thirties were a most difficult decade, and Mamamía not only had to struggle to keep the family afloat on the depression sea, she also had to make sure her sons stayed in school and graduated and got jobs. The two were irresponsible and intractable. Men were like that. The world would be a sorry place indeed without women to clear the path and keep the men on it. As the oldest woman of the clan, Mamamía was the nucleus that held the atom together, and she continued in this role until her death. After the depression and after the political upheavals that wracked Havana until 1941, when a new constitution was adopted, the family settled into a period of relative prosperity and calm that lasted until 1959. This was the year when Castro took control of the island. It was also the beginning of another family trauma: emigration and diaspora.

In the meantime, however, the compound by the Quibú was built; life was easy and bountiful. At last, it seemed, Mamamía could rest. And that she did in the best way she knew how: cooking up huge vats of Andalusian pigs' feet or Basque-style cod on Sundays for the host of visitors that stopped by, the rest of the week tending to her flowers and fruit trees and, for long hours in the afternoon, saying her rosary and reading from her breviary.

Sometimes I would sneak into her room and sit quietly on the floor by her. She prayed, I remember, in a trance, with her eyes half-closed and lips barely moving as the beads slipped through her fingers. Yet prayer was never an excuse for her to disengage from people. If interrupted, she bore it graciously and returned to her praying when matters were settled.

Hers was a goodness without fanfare and so was approachable. One could feel it, touch it, and be touched by it. For her, each dawn brought either a blessing or a curse. If the day was cursed, there was all the hope in the world that the next would be blessed; if blessed, beware lest you put too much trust in your good fortune, for there would always be tomorrow, wolf or sheep, you never knew.

Her philosophy was of the simplest sort, made clear as the tropical seas, not because she codified or preached it, but because it was her life, there for anyone to experience and to share. Even death bowed before her, liberated her to enter the rest of us, and in so doing became her final triumph over the forces of despair. Of all the people I have known, I dare call only one a saint: Mamamía, the lady with the Buddha face.

On the Beach

ON THEIR DAY off, the maid Sagrada and her husband, Manolo, took me with them to a beach on the outskirts of the city. I was used to the clubs and resort beaches in Matanzas, particularly Varadero with its pearly sand and crystal waters. This particular beach, however, was different. For one thing it was very crowded and, unlike Varadero, the people there were dark skinned and rowdy. Few of them wore swimsuits, many going into the water fully clothed or, in some cases, in their underwear. The younger children wore nothing at all. I remember the smell of food, as the beach had been turned into a giant kitchen, with families gathered round big pots filled with *moros con cristianos* (rice and black beans) and roast pork. There was music, too — guitars and the tat-tat-tat, ta-pum, tat-tat of bongos, and one naked girl, no older than four, doing the rumba to the accompaniment of her family's syncopated clapping.

It was an overcast day, and damp, so that the air was heavy and the sand cold and unpleasant to sit on. My physical discomfort was heightened by the awareness of not belonging — I was too white, too inhibited.

In order to pass the time, I occupied myself by building a medieval sand city. As I was giving shape to the large wall that surrounded the burg, a girl of fourteen or fifteen approached the water's edge. She wore a white cotton dress and walked lithely, sliding her feet and kicking up sand as she went. When she reached the waves she did not stop to test the water, nor did she make a face as people are prone to do when their toes first feel the cool sea. Rather, she kept going without missing a step as if the ocean was her element and she was returning to it after a brief foray onto solid ground. The girl reached waist-deep water then dove under. Her head surfaced a few yards away, eyes closed, and a smile parting her glazed lips. She rubbed her face with both hands and started back, her gait the same: casual, relaxed, like a tropical Nereid.

Out of the water, she paused by me to stretch her body, shake her matted hair, and comb it back with her fingers. The dress clung to her body delineating every dip and curve and swell. I was still kneeling, looking up at this beauty in white when she glanced in my direction with eyes like glinting coals. She offered a smile and disappeared into the crowd.

I could work no more. I returned to where Sagrada and Manolo were sitting and lay back on the sand to watch the gouache of clouds get darker and darker until the rain came and forced every-one off the beach.

To this day that girl is my picture of the feminine ideal and it is to her that I compare the women I know. I am the child building sand castles; she, the one braving the waves, coming back all the more beautiful for it. She smiles; she walks into the sea of bodies behind us; her interruption is a blessing on my labor.

What Happened?

I WAS IN the movies by myself and had left my seat to get a drink of water. Just as I was bending over the fountain, I heard a loud explosion. For an instant my vision blurred. I put my arm out to catch the wall, but the wall didn't fall. I heard screams, and then, faster than I ever thought I could move, I flew down the steps and was outside. A policeman ran by, gun in hand, looking in every direction, not knowing what to do or where to go. I looked at him hoping his face might offer reassurance, but he trotted down the street, dazed, his eyes mirrors to my uncertainty.

A wave of bodies spewed out the theater doors and suddenly the sidewalk was jammed with people shoving and pushing and disembodied voices all around — *¿Qué pasó? Ay Diós, ¿qué pasó?* — when I felt someone grab me by the arm and turn me around. A dimly familiar voice said, "Go home, hurry. Go home!" Looking up I recognized my cousin Dioni. I asked what had happened; she answered, "Go home!" All the time I was thinking earthquake because of the building trembling the way it did, but that made no sense: there aren't earthquakes in Havana.

As I was walking the two blocks to the bus stop, the sirens came. They filled the streets with howling and whining — arcing panic of police cars, fire trucks, ambulances. *¿Qué pasó?*

At the stop I was biding my time reconstructing the rest of the movie (I had already seen it) but my memory of it seemed rather flat, so the anxiety of waiting took over and I began to feel uncomfortable and jumpy inside as if I were too much alone. That's when I glanced up and saw in the distance a gigantic mushroom cloud rising, black and already spreading into an umbrella and now I was really confused. All along I thought the explosion had been close by. Things weren't so bad then. Or maybe they were worse. The cloud was hundreds of feet high, and I had a funny taste in my mouth, a taste of doom. I needed to know. *¿Qué pasó?*

The bus, when it came, was nearly empty. An old unshaven man several seats behind me started a conversation. I answered in monosyllables. He asked for money. I told him I had none and he got off, mumbling to himself. Almost as we reached La Playa, I saw the strangest thing — a rain of ash began to fall, lightly at first, then gradually thickening until the air was gray and the light turned an ochre yellow.

Close to my stop I pulled the cord and readied myself at the back door. As usual the bus did not stop. The driver opened the door and slowed down enough for me to jump without splattering myself against a telephone pole. I made my leap through the ash rain and landed on the run, not stopping until I made it to the house six blocks away.

My parents rushed to me while I was shaking ash out of my hair. "*¿Qué pasó?*" I asked. Sabotage, they answered. The revolutionaries blew up a munitions dump outside town. They were glad I was home. The police were picking people up randomly for questioning. I was relieved, too. It hadn't been a good day. That night I had a nightmare where the world was in my stomach and it blew up.

El Country

NOT FAR FROM where we lived, perhaps fifteen minutes by bicycle, was a neighborhood called the Country Club. Its streets were heavily shaded by almond trees, palms, and poincianas that spilled their blood-colored flowers onto the cracked sidewalks. Lining the streets on either side, except where an occasional weed-choked lot appeared, were high concrete walls topped with bottle shards. Once the walls had been white, but now time and humidity had covered them with a green layer of moss. At intervals the walls sported large cracks through which thick vines had crept. Entering El Country, which I often did alone, was like entering the stomach of decay. Forbidding, lonely, overgrown, the sun never seemed to have breached its shadows, and behind those walls, beyond the trees, I imagined vast, decaying palaces where the past lived.

More or less in the center of El Country was an artificial lake known simply as El Laguito, graced at one end with neo-Doric columns and marble steps leading nowhere in particular. White geese and swans (or do I imagine these?) floated gently on the surface yet did not allay my anxiety. No doubt, the designer must have been fond of French symbolist literature. Evocative of a dim mythical past as the little lake was, it seemed nonetheless a monstrous anomaly in the tropics, and so few people frequented it.

Other than as a minor landmark now fallen by the wayside in most *habaneros'* minds, El Laguito and its surroundings had a reputation as a dumping ground for the secret police. Every few months a body, with signs of the horrific tortures attributed to government death squads and battered beyond recognition, was found on its banks. Why the torturers chose this place to discard their victims was never clear to me. Obviously, they wanted the body to be found; yet if such was the case, they could have left it in a more conspicuous place, closer to the university, for example. Perhaps it was a message to the wealthy: not even they were exempt from the horror. The ant-filled mouths gaped at the protective walls.

Once, not long before the fall of the Batista regime, I spied a dirt path leading off the road around the lake into an empty lot. Driven by curiosity and filled with dread, I got off my bike and entered the path on foot. Burrs stuck to me and thorny vines crisscrossed the path so that I had to crouch under them. Soon I came to a clearing where the foundations of a house were still visible through the weeds. The sun shone here and it settled me. Off to one side I saw an old, half-dead tree. I walked over and stood under it. Looking up I saw a rope dangling from one of its branches. The brilliant light hurt my eyes and I lowered my sight. Around me on the ground were bones of all sizes and shapes. There were also pants and a pair of two-toned shoes. It wasn't until I picked up the largest bone and stood it up next to my leg — it was a few inches taller than my knee — that my mind clicked and forced me to confront the dreadful question: Was this a human bone I was holding? I stood motionless, my body teeming with more emotions than I could possibly manage, but I did not panic. I dropped the bone and walked back as calmly as I had come in, being careful not to rip my clothes on the vines.

The questions stayed with me on the way and for a few days after. Eventually, I told two of my cousins about it. Being older than I, they laughed, claiming I was imagining things as usual. When I said I could lead them to the place, they excused themselves and quickly changed the conversation.

When I think of hell, I visualize not fire and darkness and agonizing souls, but El Country — its empty streets, its thick vegetable soul and high walls, and El Laguito with its smell of death.

Chivato

NEXT TO A *marijuanero,* or pothead, the worst thing one could be in Havana in 1958 was an informer, a *chivato.* For the most part the *chivato* informed not out of allegiance to the Batista government — such a motive might have been understandable to most people, and admirable to a few — but for much baser reasons. He did it for the few pieces of silver the police might throw at him; he did it out of cowardice: to say no to the secret police might have made him an accomplice to the revolution; he did it out of hatred and envy of those whom he knew personally: coworkers, an ex-employer who might have fired him, casual acquaintances whose lives were orderly and prosperous. For the true *chivato* was not a passive listener. He used the worms of friendship and affability to hook people on the line to the nearest interrogation center. He made his elephant ears available to friends' confidences, and his words, complicitous and encouraging, pulled out the compromising statements.

To do this required a certain amount of social dexterity. *Habaneros* were aware that *chivatos* could be found anywhere people congregated: in bars, in cafés, on the beach. Open political discussions were never held in such places. Only in the womb of the family or among intimate friends could one speak one's mind. Children were taught not to talk politics in school (a warning we often ignored). Your political ideas reflected your parents', and walls, schoolyards, urinals had ears. You never knew . . .

So the *chivato* had to break through the mistrust. He might appear to sympathize with the revolutionary forces, or at least complain about the corruption of Batista and his cadres; he might seek someone's understanding and pity by relating family or work problems over a drink; he might build the friendship more casually through *cubilete,* the dice game traditionally played where men gathered; or he might invite the "friend" to those places where men bared all — the whorehouses of the city. And throughout the process, the *chivato* dropped the offhand political remark, subtly and innocently worded in hopes that it might unlock the door to the other man's politics. The *chivato*'s patience and insistence were of mythical proportions. Too often they worked.

By 1958 anti-Batista forces were making significant military gains against the government. The rebels in the Escambray and Sierra Maestra mountains became increasingly venturesome in their attacks on the poorly trained and all but demoralized regular army. In Havana, activists mobilized the students in frequent strikes and marches. The consequences of participation in these actions were none too pleasant: imprisonment, torture, death. Nevertheless the young, fueled by revolutionary fervor, stepped up their activities. Every schoolboy could sing the revolution's battle hymn, "Adelante cubanos." Opposition spread to the not-so-young who, fed up with corruption and repression, helped quietly in the background by providing money, food, and medical supplies to those struggling for "freedom and democracy" in the mountains.

The government saw the whole country turning against it and was powerless to stem the tide. In its frustration, it unleashed its dogs on the populace. Everyone was suspect. The police arrested journalists, machine guns mowed down demonstrators, corpses appeared in pools of blood on streetcorners. And the *chivatos* were as plentiful as flies. The word of the weak was pitted against the word of the strong.

My father had a friend who became a victim of a *chivato.* A salesman, he was an extroverted and friendly man with little, if any, interest in politics. Across the street from where he worked there was a bar he would frequent during his lunch hour to have a beer or two and to talk shop with colleagues. Among them was a young clerk who attended these reunions religiously. The older men did not pay much attention to him, thinking him an ambitious fellow eager to learn the tricks of the trade from seasoned professionals. They talked to him, joked with him, bought him drinks. My father's friend, outgoing as he was, befriended the clerk, and soon the youngster was at his heels, changing the topic from selling to politics. He requested a contribution for the cause. The salesman waved him off. He was not interested in politics. The clerk asked again a week later and was once more turned down, but rather than giving up, the young man became more insistent, bringing up the matter on an almost daily basis. Finally one day, when the salesman was in a particularly bad mood, the clerk made a request and the older man responded, "Look, I already gave some. Leave me alone."

That's all the *chivato* needed. He had him. That same night, the police dragged the salesman away from his home. His wife, who had received no answer from the agents as to where they were taking her husband, called my father immediately. It would fall squarely on him to find the salesman, for my father had some *palanca*.

Now the practice of *palanca* was a custom deeply entrenched in Cuban society. The word itself means lever, but in a social sense it referred to influence, a contact within a particular institution who might help you when you needed it. In business, a *palanca* was instrumental in making a sale or getting a contract signed; in politics, you couldn't go anywhere without it; with the police, it was the only reasonably certain way of getting someone out of trouble. "Give me a point of balance and a lever strong enough," said Archimedes, "and I can move the world." In Cuba, the higher up your acquaintance, the stronger your leverage. In a society where laws and regulations were considered obstacles rather than aids to everyday living and social advancement, having a *palanca* or two constituted a significant advantage. For this reason, I never had any difficulty in understanding Archimedes' principle.

Although most societies (no matter how legalistic and puritanical they might be in their fervor to apply legal principles equally to all its members) are always open to the corruption of influence, it is usually the rich and powerful who benefit from it.

In Cuba, you did not have to be either of these things to have leverage simply because *palanca* was based on friendship, and friendship was more important than law. Friends were made in school
or in the neighborhood or a bar or a whorehouse. Once estab-
lished, friendship was a force that held people together, akin to
the force that holds atoms together. No matter how far life might
separate any two friends, the bond was still there (given that the
relationship had not been violated). When one of the pair tugged
for help, the other was bound to answer. Another principle of
physics was thus made clear to me.

My father was not wealthy, nor was he influential. He had a
good job that allowed us a secure but modest middle-class life.
Our surname, Medina, was as common as you can find and had
none of the status or prestige necessary to open doors. But he did
have two friends who could help him get the salesman out of police hands.

One was a fellow he had gone to school with and was now an
officer in the army. He had not much influence by himself, but his
father had been a colonel, and the mere mention of his name was
enough to break through the inertia with which appeals for consideration were routinely treated. The second was an eccentric
police captain who drove around the city in a late-model convert-
ible with his pet lion in the back seat. Given these last details, it is
safe to deduce that he was not the most honest captain in the city,
official salaries being what they were and that branch of public
service being notoriously corrupt. But he was a good friend and
would help my father.

Dealing with political arrests was no easy matter. First of all,
they tended to occur at night when it was most difficult to reach
someone who might intercede. No doubt the arresters were aware
that the suspect might have a *palanca* and so waited until after
10 P.M., then acted quickly, never revealing to family members
where the person was being taken. Second, it wasn't always clear
who was doing the arresting. The agents might be members of the
army, the regular police, or, if the person happened to be especially unfortunate, the secret police. To further complicate matters, each police station recruited its own *chivatos* and, unless the
suspect was well known, it acted independently without consult-

ing or informing the bureaucracy. Often, the arresting agents drove across precinct lines to get at a suspect and did not bother to tell the local force. Thus, inquiries regarding the person's whereabouts, more often than not, led nowhere as the officer in charge at that station might have no knowledge of the arrest. If by chance he did know, he was under no obligation to tell. Furthermore, political detainees were never booked, thus the arrest action was never official. It was easier that way: the less paperwork, the less delay. Besides, without records, the responsibility was much more difficult to trace to a specific individual or station. In Cuba even the police disregarded the law.

The object of the arrests was twofold. First, the presumed sympathizer might provide important information. If that person was merely giving money or food to the rebels, he had to hand it to someone who was directly involved in the movement. Second, those responsible for the arrest and interrogation were forever hopeful that their superiors might reward them for a job well done. Toward the end of Batista's rule, however, this hope was more a fantasy. There were too many revolutionaries, too many sympathizers. Detaining one became no more important than catching a petty thief.

Batista's ship was going under, everyone knew that. Yet the interrogations and the torture continued. It seemed as if the government forces, facing a defeat that became more and more certain with every passing day, and in their own way understanding the inevitability of history in the flesh of Fidel Castro, Che Guevara, Raúl Castro, and their *barbudos* — Davids against a gangrenous Goliath — released the force of their frustration upon the suspects they picked up on an almost daily basis. Arrest and torture became ends in themselves. It didn't matter whether the detainee was guilty or not. If the interrogators did not receive the answers they wanted, they resorted to the most medieval means of extracting confessions: beatings, nail pullings, castration. In turn, their brutality, now more meaningless than ever, radically alienated a significant segment of the middle class whose children bore the brunt of the government's tactics.

How my father did it I never found out. I remember that, once he heard from the salesman's wife, he made a series of phone calls, then left the house and did not return until early the next morning. His friend had been released with only a few bruises to show for his ordeal. My father and his contacts had mobilized quickly enough so that the interrogation had been stopped before going too far. The salesman had learned his lesson and through him we all had. Even the merest suggestion of solidarity with the rebels meant complicity. Silence and seeming political indifference were essential.

It is curious that once the Revolution triumphed and the new system started functioning, the *chivato* as a type disappeared, but informing did not. On the contrary, it became institutionalized. While, before, informers were recruited from the shards at the periphery of society, now it became the duty of every citizen to uncover counterrevolutionary activity. To this end, the new regime organized neighborhood committees, the main purpose of which was to ensure that people living within a prescribed area were acting in accordance with the principles of the Revolution. Any and all suspicious goings-on, such as gatherings of several people for any reason other than forming revolutionary cells, late night visits by strangers, grumblings at food lines, bringing wrapped packages into one's house, eating well or dressing better than others on the block (signs of trading on the black market), were to be reported and investigated, and the neighbor involved was to explain himself before the group. If his answers were not satisfactory to the committee, then higher authorities, namely the G-2, the new secret police, took over.

Before 1959, Cubans were characteristically extroverted and congenial. One's home was one's most prized possession, but it was always offered to visitors with the greeting, "*Ésta es tu casa.*" After the Revolution, one's house became a cave — dark, forbidding, solitary. Let's have no visitors. Let's shut our blinds lest someone see us cooking the chicken we bought from a farmer outside town. Let's not dress too smartly or seem too happy. Even in the cave, watch out. Your children have been taught in the new schools that the Revolution is above all — home, family, filial love. They may overhear your criticisms, your complaints about life in a society where drabness, boredom, and lack of incentive are the norms and may turn you in. In so doing, they will perform the ultimate sacrifice. "Within the Revolution, everything; without the Revolution, nothing."

The new system has gone so far as to decree that those people charged with counterrevolutionary thoughts and actions make public confessions accepting charges against them as a way of showing atonement. This has been the case with many writers and artists who have refused to follow the dictates of the state: they suffer the ultimate debasement, they become their own *chivatos*.

In such a situation the individual has little choice but to turn inward and to put on a hard, expressionless mask (any show of emotion toward anything other than the state and its leaders might be misconstrued as sedition). The eyes turn ashen and glazed like a lizard's. They become slits that nothing breaches, not even the sun, and they show only a wary defensiveness bred of fear, solitude, and hopelessness without respite.

The Cuban character is dying a slow but sure death, and in its place the character of the New Man will appear. But this New Man will not be new — he will already exist in Russia, Poland, Czechoslovakia, and the other countries of Eastern Europe — and he is to be bred of humiliation, bitterness, and puritanical Marxist zeal so antithetical to the Cuban sun and the Cuban sky. The *chivato* will, in the end, have won.

Leaving

5 A.M., JANUARY 1, 1959, my father rushed into my grandmother's bedroom where I had stayed the night. At first, still in the grip of dreams, I saw him through a haze, his face flushed, eyes round and open. He waved his arms and his mouth was moving, but I couldn't, at that instant between sleep and wakedom, make out what he was saying. In a few seconds, his words had broken through my slumber. "*¡Cayó Batista!*" "Batista fell!"

I jumped out of bed and rushed out to the backyard where someone, I think my great-aunt Lolita, embraced me and pointed out my state of undress. When I came back out, the whole family was cheering and dancing, giving thanks to God that the tyrant had, at long last, been deposed. It was a day of rejoicing, of reveling in a collective hope shared by most that things would be good now, that peace had come and corruption had been eradicated. Such feelings I have never since experienced: a bit like drunkenness, yet lighter than that and clearer, like the warm air of that beautiful day, shared by all.

Eventually we found ourselves in Mamamía's living room watching T.V. and listening on the radio to the latest news reports. The men drank, the women gabbed, the phone rang incessantly with the news everyone knew already, as if it needed repeating over and over to make it real. The craziness spilled over onto the following week and no one bothered to go to work. The whole city was engulfed in the celebration. Patriotic banners appeared everywhere. People smiled. At times one would hear a shout coming from a car driving by or from a stranger across the street: "*¡Viva Fidel! ¡Viva Cuba Libre!*" Throughout the week we awaited the arrival of the rebels into the capital.

Not all were glad of the change. Some were *batistianos* — Batista supporters who believed the man had accomplished many good things for the nation and had given order and prosperity to a people who sorely needed them, no matter that he was corrupt and despotic. Others did not trust this young man, this Fidel Castro. It was difficult to know what he stood for; he was a bit too fond of slogans like "*Armas, ¿para qué?*" and of dim terms, such as *freedom* and *democracy;* he also seemed inebriated by the adulation he met as he traveled westward in his victory march. "He postures too much as a messiah," "The people are too enamored of him," they would say. Above all, these skeptics were very much troubled by the rumors that Castro was a Marxist and that he would lead the country directly to Russia's door. Finally, there was the group of those who had profited directly through their association with Batista: lawyers, politicians, architects, military men, whose lives and fortunes were suddenly endangered. They plotted ways of leaving the country and taking their wealth. Most embittered, they saw only their losses, closed doors and windows, planned their escape. The disenchanted ones, however, were in the minority for now. Their voices were drowned out in the quasi-Dionysian chaos of the following weeks. They sat in dark corners and grumbled.

Fidel Castro arrived in Havana on January 8 at the head of a column of *barbudos,* or bearded ones. With him were el Che, his brother Raúl, Camilo Cienfuegos, and all the mythic figures who had fought in the Sierra Maestra. For a boy like myself, whose dreams fed on the feats of warriors struggling against evil, the appearance of the triumphant bearded ones on the streets of my city was the ultimate confirmation that heroes existed beyond the pages of adventure novels.

The whole city turned out to greet them. Women and children crowded round to kiss, to touch, to embrace them. Seeing a rebel on the street was enough to make the heart jump, for they were viewed with an awe bordering on the reverence reserved for saints. These were, after all, our young liberators and they looked the part. Their long hair tied in pony tails, their black berets, their olive green uniforms, and their gun belts were to set the style for many a "revolutionary" of the future. Around their necks hung rosaries, religious medals, scapulae, and other mementos given to them by thankful citizens on their march to Havana. These were the wild men who had redeemed us and in their eyes glowed the future with an intensity evident only among those who have struggled with history.

Along with the revolutionary fervor, and perhaps a direct result of it, there arose in Havana a cult of things military. People started collecting relics of the Revolution — souvenirs of battles they had never witnessed, of a life they had never lived. The most prized of these were the ones given away by the *barbudos* — berets, gun belts, bullets, and even live grenades. Next best was to purchase the wares from street vendors who had astutely put away their costume jewelry and cheap toys and now dealt in war objects. Buying them, however, was akin to cheating — for all one knew one was buying goods made in Japan. I myself was the object of envy of many friends because I had collected three bullets from three different *barbudos.* One in particular, which I kept swaddled in thick cotton and exhibited with great ceremony, piqued their awe — a live .50-caliber still capable of taking any one of our young heads off.

Within days of Fidel's arrival, the first of what was to become a series of ominous and revelatory signs appeared. Although many of Batista's men had escaped on the days immediately preceding and following the fall, many others not high enough in the hierarchy to be aware of the situation remained behind and were subsequently captured by the revolutionary forces. On these men — police captains, army colonels, and a few members of the political bureaucracy — fell the weight of the new "justice."

Of the many military tribunals that were televised during this period I remember only one distinctly, that of Colonel Sosa Blanco. Sosa Blanco's main crime, the tragic flaw that was to lead ineluctably to his end, was that, as colonel in the Cuban army, he had pursued and engaged the rebel forces in the mountains. He was charged with acts of torture, cold-blooded assassinations of innocent peasants, and other crimes against the Cuban people. In spite of the several dozen witnesses that testified before the court and the T.V. cameras, no charge was ever substantiated. In addition, the colonel was not allowed a lawyer, nor was he given the opportunity to speak in his own defense. He stood, I recall, before the judges, and behind him the rabble packing the gallery interrupted the proceedings with the latest slogans and with the refrain, *Pa-re-dón, Pa-re-dón* (Firing squad! Firing squad!).

At first the colonel stood proudly, facing, no, challenging his captors. As the trial progressed, as more and more of the witnesses brought new charges and as the audience's lust for his death grew, the colonel drooped. Where once his face was raised in arrogance, now it looked shadowy and troubled. Slowly I saw it soften, go from disdain to anger to befuddlement. Then for an instant the light of discovery graced it, but the light was flooded over by the swift realization that he was a condemned man and that his sentence had been passed the moment he'd been captured. He was not on trial here; he was on display. In the end his eyes turned into ashen pits, contorted, twitching, almost like a child's who knows no mercy will come his way.

I did not know whether the charges were true. All the adults around me were dismayed, and so I concurred, giving the man the benefit of my outrage. Sosa Blanco was hardly an honorable man, I found that out later, but what greater punishment did a man deserve than this public humiliation, this dragging of his character in the mud of collective hatred and vengeance? The colonel was executed a few days after the trial, and that too was aired on T.V., but I did not watch. I had had enough. I believed the Revolution to be white and a darkness was creeping in with which I was incapable of coping.

Television, the great filler of my time, was beginning to change. Before Castro it had been solely an entertainment medium; now, along with the trials, aired for the most part during the first three months of the Revolution, there were Fidel's epic policy speeches, and soap operas laden with revolutionary and Marxist motifs.

In the mornings there were children's shows that appeared at first to be little different from prerevolution ones. As before, a teacher figure talked, sang, and played with a group of youngsters. The emcees in the new programs, however, were quite young and serious minded. They wore army fatigues or militia uniforms and never smiled except when extolling the new system. Then a beatific look came over their faces as if they had personally witnessed what History had prepared for those who loved the Revolution. Besides discussing agrarian reform, the distribution of private property, and other topics that I could only label as profoundly boring, these paramilitary teachers, whose humor had been gobbled up by their zeal (the Revolution allowed fun no quarter), often went on violent tirades against the *yanquis.*

It appeared that the emcees found in that term a synonym for evil. In one such show, the host, a young uniformed woman with hair tied back in a pony tail *a la barbudo,* was involved in an extended tirade against imperialist oppression when a boy in the group spoke up, wanting her to clarify a point she was making. She looked indignantly at the boy and said, "Don't ever speak without raising your hand. You don't want to be like the *yanquis,* do you?" The boy's lower lip quivered and his face darkened with shame. He had been labeled before the world and his peers: *Yanqui! Outcast! Pariah!*

It took a long while before the shadows of television and what they represented deterred my euphoria. That medium is flat and as such distancing, tingeing real events with unreality. Fantasy is much more powerful, and my fantasy colored everything I saw. The heroes were still glorious: Fidel, strong and determined; Che, with the fierce eyes and soft, convincing smile; Raúl, the quiet one, waiting in the wings. There were also the great projects on hand and dreams that spread beyond the island to all of America.

After a time the novelty passed. Daily life went on for me not much differently than before. I went to school, swam on the beach, read, dreamed, felt lonely, bored, excited. But the cracks in the shining globe of the Revolution multiplied and widened. Newspapers were expropriated; the opposition, afraid of the consequences of speaking up, left the island; all private schools were taken over by a bureaucracy more intent on indoctrinating than educating.

All about me people talked in whispers. My parents looked glum and asked about school and what we were taught. Friends started leaving, to Miami, Mexico, Spain. Soon family reunions stopped. They were too risky. Freedom had been given and taken away again. This was no dream. The future was the past, except less carefree, less warm, heavier with doctrine and dim visions of a society modeled too far away from our shores: a different sort of yoke. I, like the rest of my family, turned my back on the Revolution. Little did I know that in doing so I would forfeit the place of my birth.

We left on one of the last regularly scheduled flights from Havana. There were tears and embraces with those we left behind. The bitter apple I had swallowed left a lump in my throat that made it difficult to breathe. As we were boarding, my great-uncle Luis took a photograph of us on the boarding ladder, which I still have in my possession. The four of us are smiling and waving. We expected to return in a few months. The months turned to years and our hope was blown away.

The gray snow of disenchantment began to fall over my city and my childhood. The past was fixed in place; fate had conspired to cut me off from it. Suddenly I was surrounded by ice, and I jumped into the white mounds with all the enthusiasm I could muster. I renounced allegiance to the country of my birth when I became an American citizen, yet the blood still pulled and memory called. Thus it was that I became two persons, one a creature of warmth, the other the snow swimmer. The first would be forever a child dancing to the beat of the waves; the second was the adult, striving to emerge from the river of cold — invigorated, wise, at peace with life.

The truism that no one can ever go home again becomes a special predicament for the young exile: my childhood lies inside the bowl of distance and politics, unapproachable and thus disconnected from my adulthood. The two revolve around each other like twin stars, pulling and tugging, without hope of reconciliation. Everywhere I see Fate smiling the smile of the Sphynx. I could bemoan my state at the hands of the indifferent creature and thus belie a need for control of my life, which is illusion. Instead, I remember the family, their craziness, their resilience, their collective tongue wagging wildly at despair, and I too smile.

They have given me a home made of materials nothing but death can breach.

As long as there is blood in my veins, as long as there are words on my tongue, stories to be told, the house stands and leans freely into the future. Whatever winds may come, welcome.

Glossary

abuelo: grandfather.

"Adelante Cubanos": "Forward, Cubans," the hymn of the 26th of July Movement.

anón: a custard apple.

arboleda: a grove of trees.

Armas, ¿para qué?: What purpose arms?

Ay, Dios, ¿qué pasó?: Oh, God, what happened?

barbudos: bearded ones; the name given the revolutionaries who fought alongside Fidel Castro in the Sierra Maestra and Escambray mountains.

barracones: the living quarters for cane cutters; they were modeled on slave quarters and were not much more comfortable.

batey: the grounds of a *colonia* or sugar plantation; originally, a Taíno or Siboney settlement.

batistiano: a supporter of Batista.

bohío: the typical thatched-roof dwelling of the Cuban countryside.

botero: a collective taxi.

cafetero: a coffee vendor.

café con leche: warm milk with coffee; the French call it café au lait.

caimito: a star apple; a fruit with purple interior out of which oozes a milky juice; eating it is a quasi-erotic experience.

"Canción del Pirata": "Song of the Pirate," a poem by the Spanish Romantic José de Espronceda.

carbonero: a charcoal maker.

Carretera Central: the Central Highway; Cuba's most important highway, it runs west to east.

carretero: a teamster.

caudillo: a leader or strongman.

Cayó Batista: Batista fell.

ceiba: a massive tropical tree of the silk-cotton family.

chipojo: a large chameleon usually found in cow pastures and banana groves.

chivato: an informer.

chorizo: a type of sausage.

colonia: a sugar plantation.

colono: a sugar farmer.

cubilete: a dice game traditionally played in bars.

cucurucho de maní: a paper cone filled with hot peanuts.

dale: hit it.

despojo: a quick exorcism of an evil spirit or curse.

empanada: a meat turnover; the Cuban version is deep fried.

El Caballero de París: the Gentleman of Paris; the name given to one of the street characters of Havana.

El Country: short for Country Club, an exclusive neighborhood in prerevolutionary Havana.

El Laberinto de los Espejos: literally, the Labyrinth of Mirrors; the name given the house of mirrors in an amusement park in Havana.

El Laguito: Little Lake.

"El Mundo en Televisión": "The World on Television," the name given a television program that featured Grandfather Pablo.

Ese Carlos es la pata del diablo: That Carlos is the devil's hoof.

Ésta es tu casa: This is your house — a common greeting after welcoming a visitor into one's home; Fidel took it literally.

frita: the Cuban version of the hamburger, usually sold in stalls on the street; my Uncle Carlos once told me that the best were made of dog meat, but, no doubt, he was joking.

guao: a terebinthine tree, the leaves of which cause a mean rash when touched.

guaracha: a type of Cuban music that makes the hips swing freely and the spirit fly; it is a direct precursor of salsa, and some

people claim that, except for orchestration, there is no difference between the two.

guarapo: sugarcane juice; it sweetens the blood and is quite re-
freshing with crushed ice.

guataquero: a hoer.

guayabal: a grove of guava trees.

guayabera: the traditional Cuban shirt, made of cotton or silk
(polyester is an aberration); it was invented in Oriente province in the eighteenth century and — allow me this bit of chau-
vinism — then spread throughout the Spanish-speaking world.

habanero: a resident of Havana.

Hondón: the name given a low-lying cow pasture in La Luisa.

ingenio: a machine or contraption; in our case, a sugar mill.

Jardines: the name of my great-uncle Octavio's plantation; literally, gardens.

La Charada: the Cuban version of the numbers game, based on
Chinese numerology.

"La Bolsa del Saber": "The Bag of Knowledge"; the name given to
the question-and-answer program in which my grandfather
and great-uncle participated.

La Cadena Azul: the first, and best-known, radio network in Cuba.

La Luisa: my Grandfather Fiquito's farm.

La Playa: literally, the beach; the name given to a popular beach
just west of Havana.

La Quinta Avenida: Fifth Avenue; a major thoroughfare, which
ran from Havana to the newer suburbs to the west.

La Rampa: a fashionable business and shopping area in Havana.

liceo: a lyceum or town club; often the scene of dances and heated
political meetings.

Llanura Roja: the Red Plain; an area in the southern part of
Matanzas province.

Los Tigres de Masferrer: the Tigers of Masferrer; the name given
to a squad of marauding henchmen led by Masferrer, a supporter of Batista.

machetero: a sugarcane cutter, so named because he wields a
machete.

malecón: a breakwater in the form of a wall that ran along the
length of the Havana waterfront.

mambises: the Cuban freedom fighters who fought for independence from Spain.

mamey: a tropical fruit, shaped somewhat like a small football, with red, stringy meat and a dark, shiny pit.

mamoncillo: honey berry; a small fruit consisting of a large pit surrounded by a bittersweet pulp; generally, it is popped whole into the mouth and sucked until the pulp is gone.

manicero: a peanut vendor; also the name of a famous song written by Moisés Simons.

Matanzas: a province directly to the east of Havana province; the word literally means slaughters.

Medinadas: the title of Grandfather Pablo's only book; literally, it means Medinities.

mondongo: entrails or tripe; you'd be surprised what delights can be concocted from the innards of an animal.

montaña rusa: roller coaster.

moros con cristianos: Moors and Christians; black beans and rice, the traditional Cuban dish, so named because black beans (*moros*) are mixed with the rice (*cristianos*) to form a delicious, nutritious, and racially balanced combination.

Nochebuena: Christmas Eve, the most important holiday in Cuba.

palanca: lever.

pan con lechón: a sandwich made from roast pig on which has been dribbled *mojito,* a dressing made with lard, lemon juice, garlic, and cooked onions.

pañuelo: handkerchief.

papa rellena: a ball of mashed potatoes with ground beef in the center, which is then rolled in bread crumbs and deep fried.

paredón: a large, thick wall, especially that against which a condemned person is executed by firing squad.

Paseo del Prado: a stately boulevard in old Havana.

pastel: any kind of pastry; it is most often filled with ground beef or guava paste.

pícaro: a rascal, the most famous of which is not my Uncle Carlos but Lazarillo de Tormes.

Por ahí voy: There I go.

puerco: hog.

quimbumbia: a game similar to baseball, played with two sticks. One, sharpened on both ends, is placed on the ground and hit at one end with the bat. As the stick twirls in mid-air, it is hit again toward the opposing team, who try to catch it.

"Río Manzanares": a song in which the narrator has to cross a swollen river in order to reach his mother's side.

romana: an enclosed station used for weighing sugarcane wagons and trucks.

Sal de aquí, viejo sinvergüenza: Get out of here, you dirty old man.

santera: a witch doctor who often doubles as a herbalist and healer.

Se armó el acabose: This is the end.

solar: the name given in Cuba to a tenement.

"Soy Abuelo": "I am a Grandfather," a selection from Grandfather Pablo's *Medinadas.*

Taínos: also called Arawaks, the Taínos were the Indians who inhabited the Greater Antilles. By the end of the sixteenth century they had been purportedly exterminated in Cuba.

tío: uncle.

un loco: a lunatic.

yanquis: Yankees.

zafra: the sugarcane harvest.

zapote: sapodilla, the fruit of the marmalade tree; it has a rough, brown skin and grayish, stringy pulp; in spite of its appearance, it is quite tasty.